INDUSTRIAL INTELLIGENCE

INDUSTRIAL INTELLIGENCE

The Executive's Guide for
Making Informed Commercial
Real Estate Decisions

JUSTIN SMITH

COPYRIGHT © 2021 JUSTIN SMITH
All rights reserved.

INDUSTRIAL INTELLIGENCE
The Executive's Guide for Making Informed Commercial Real Estate Decisions

ISBN 978-1-5445-1993-7 *Hardcover*
978-1-5445-1992-0 *Paperback*
978-1-5445-1991-3 *Ebook*
978-1-5445-1994-4 *Audiobook*

CONTENTS

INTRODUCTION 9
1. THE US INDUSTRIAL REAL ESTATE MARKET 17
2. SITUATIONAL AWARENESS 41
3. THINKING STRATEGICALLY 49
4. REDESIGN YOUR ENVIRONMENT 63
5. TEAM AND TIMELINE 77
6. ENGAGE THE MARKET 117
7. PROPOSALS AND PROJECTIONS 129
8. TAILOR-MADE LEASES 153
9. TENANT IMPROVEMENTS AND CONSTRUCTION 173
10. WAREHOUSE OPTIMIZATION 191
11. TRANSITIONING SEAMLESSLY 219
12. ONGOING SUPPORT 231
13. ACHIEVING SCALE 243
14. TAKING INVESTMENTS TO THE NEXT LEVEL 253
CONCLUSION 267

INTRODUCTION

The high-end shopping mall of the past has now been replaced by warehouses and delivery trucks. Business giants like Facebook, Amazon, Apple, Google, and Netflix are shaping virtually every industry. Artificial intelligence, machine learning, and automation are on the rise.

It has never been more challenging to be an executive making decisions about industrial property than it is today. Manufacturing, production, distribution, and fulfillment have all changed significantly in the last decade, with their progress shaping the future of work. Industrial buildings—just six-sided boxes with four walls, a roof, and a foundation—can lead to magical outcomes for companies. After all, within these four walls, the e-commerce revolution has transformed business as we know it. They are where Tesla builds its all-electric self-driving cars with robotic arms on assembly lines. They are where Apple builds the world's finest computers, the ones that are just as beautiful on the inside as they are on the outside. And they make it possible for Amazon to deliver virtually any item we need quickly, from distribution centers located in every major city.

But before these magical outcomes could happen, these companies had to find the right buildings. They had to consider location, size, and cost. They had to see empty warehouses and imagine their potential. They had to stand exactly where you do today.

As the leader of a business that relies on industrial property, you too face numerous decisions. What kind of building will support the growth your business has planned for the next decade? Should you renew your lease, or should you move elsewhere? What experts will you need to transform a vacant building into the heart of your business? These are tough, expensive decisions, involving large amounts of money and hours of employees' time. Smart real estate choices can contribute to the success of your business, while poor decisions can spell disaster.

You have already made a smart choice by picking up this book. I am a longtime industrial real estate broker, and I have guided hundreds of executives through the same process you are embarking upon. In this book, I will walk you through the time-tested processes I use to guide executives toward informed real estate decisions to help their company thrive.

TIMELESS PRINCIPLES

First, I will break down the different industrial property markets. I will give you a quick snapshot of major trends, the latest technology, and the major players. I will discuss how your knowledge of each of these factors can help you best manage your real estate footprint.

I will lay out the types of businesses that utilize industrial properties: third-party logistics, e-commerce, food and beverage, automotive and aerospace, medical supply, life science, and more. Each business has different demand drivers accelerating in today's economy and changing landscape. However, all businesses require the same fundamental principles for their real estate projects, regardless of industry and circumstance.

Amazon CEO Jeff Bezos, who runs the most prolific e-commerce business in history, told *Forbes* magazine, "If you want to build a successful, sustainable business, don't ask yourself what could change in the next ten years that could affect your company. Instead, ask yourself what won't change, and then put all your energy and effort into those things."

In real estate, all leaders require a high-performance team, the best possible lease economics, the perfect property fit, and a seamless transition into their new space. Getting there is a long, complex process—one that I have assembled, battle-tested, and refined over several decades with the help of my colleagues and an elite group of trusted partners.

I will share valuable lessons from trusted collaborators in project management, technology, moving, architecture, and more. I will walk you through the process of assessing your current environment, brainstorming future plans, and planning your next real estate move. I will discuss who should be on your project team and guide you through creating a successful project timeline. Then I will illustrate how to best engage the market, prepare your letter(s) of intent, and negotiate a lease that is a win for everyone.

I have devoted an entire chapter to tenant improvements and all of the warehouse-specific improvements you will need to incorporate into your industrial property. I have included checklists for moving into your new facility, expectations for ongoing support, and a platform for how to scale your operations. I have even thrown in a primer for those leaders who want to take their industrial real estate skills even further and become investors.

Think of this book as a manual of strategies and tactics you can reference when you run into a challenge and are unsure of how to proceed. The word "intelligence" is important in the title of this book because the definition of intelligence, "the ability to acquire and apply knowledge and skills," truly sums up how a team of real estate professionals can help executives make informed decisions.

What will become abundantly clear throughout this book is that there is no right or wrong way to acquire industrial property for your business. There is only a *better* way than the last time. Real estate is what author Simon Sinek calls an "infinite game." As Sinek wrote in his book *The Infinite Game*, "In finite games, like football or chess, the players are known, the rules are fixed, and the endpoint is clear. The winners and losers are easily identified. In infinite games, like business or politics or life itself, the players come and go, the rules are changeable, and there is no defined endpoint. There are no winners or losers in an infinite game; there is only ahead and behind."

WHY LISTEN TO ME?

As a broker, I specialize in keeping executives ahead in the infinite game of commercial real estate. The best way I can describe my role is with an analogy from Ryan Holiday's *Ego Is the Enemy*, where he describes a person in the old Roman patronage system called the *anteambulo*, a word that translates to "clearing the path." An *anteambulo* always preceded their patron. They cleared the path, communicated messages, and generally made the patron's life easier.

Like that *anteambulo*, my job is to mesh my knowledge and skills with your organization and vision, and then walk the path with you. Like all commercial real estate brokers, I work entirely on commission. That means if there is no solution and agreement, I receive no compensation. My team only succeeds when you, the client, succeed. My favorite quote from JJ Watt, defensive end for the Houston Texans, sums this up perfectly: "Success isn't owned, it is rented, and rent is due every day."

My career spans more than five hundred real estate transactions, encompassing 5 million square feet of property and roughly half a billion dollars in value. I have worked with multiple Fortune 500 firms, public companies, large privately held companies, and high-net-worth individuals. I regularly work with C-suite executives on multifaceted projects, and I am always challenged to keep increasing the value I can bring to the table. Many of my clients helped me create this book, and I am honored.

My firm, Lee & Associates, started four decades ago with just a few small offices in Orange County, California, and has since expanded into sixty offices throughout North America, with partners in the UK and other European countries. I started with the firm sixteen years ago as an assistant and moved up the ranks to my current role as senior vice president and principal. I have a vested interest in the firm's success, and I have the ability to help shape the company's policies and platforms to best accommodate our clients' needs. I am now part of Lee & Associates' Corporate Solutions practice group, which is laser-focused on providing companies with consistent high-level execution of real estate transactions in every place they do business.

I am also part of the Society of Industrial and Office Realtors (SIOR), an organization made up of top-performing leaders in their respective markets. SIOR members collectively share best practices and creative solutions to handle the complexities industrial real estate clients will face. Through SIOR, I am able to constantly connect with top talent, which helps me uncover market intelligence and find local brokers in every market for my clients.

Lastly, my education spans from the study of economics at the University of California, Irvine, to obtaining my Master of Business Administration and my Master of Real Estate Development at the University of Southern California. These institutions, leaders in real estate education, taught me the three pillars of my practice: the inner workings of the economy, corporate functions, and real estate development.

WHAT THIS BOOK IS NOT

This book is *not* about being a landlord. Unlike most real estate books out there, it focuses entirely on the perspective of the tenant. If you only want to be an investor, this book is not for you, unless you are looking for insight into the challenges your customers are facing.

NEXT STEPS

Like any good book, you cannot dive headfirst into a nuanced discussion without some historical perspective. We will spend the first chapter going over a background of the industrial real estate market in North America and the three biggest trends shaping its future. You will not need to remember how many square feet of warehouse buildings are available or what the vacancy rate is in every city. Knowing how we reached this point in the market, however, will open your mind to different ways to think about your own projects.

CHAPTER 1

THE US INDUSTRIAL REAL ESTATE MARKET

I love to run marathons, plus another five miles. My favorite distance to run is fifty kilometers, which is roughly thirty-one miles, and I like running mountain races in lower-elevation mountain ranges. I race in the Pacific Northwest and British Columbia: I have run through the Tillamook Forest of Oregon and up and down mountains in Washington, Vancouver, and throughout the Canadian Rockies. Coming from sea level in Southern California, it can be a rude awakening to run at higher elevations without suitable acclimation time.

Each race requires extensive due diligence. I have to build a proper training plan with a running coach. I have to refine my race day plan of attack. But the most important planning steps come months before any of this: I take stock of all of the available races and comb over all the elevation profiles, seasonal temperatures, predator populations, river crossings, and more. This gives me a high-level perspective that always pays dividends on race day.

The same is true for commercial real estate—it is important to plan. Before we embark on your company's real estate journey, I want to offer you a background of the national industrial market that will give you some high-level perspective. Here you will gain an introduction and better understanding of the market's major trends, geographic submarket comparisons, and prevalent industry trends.

KEY MARKET METRICS

The *2020 CoStar United States Industrial Inventory Report* calculated the United States industrial market to be 17 billion square feet. To put this into perspective, if the total amount of industrial space were all consolidated into one gigantic warehouse, it would cover the entirety of Los Angeles and all of its four million residents under one roof. There is literally 52 square feet of warehouse space for every person in the country.

The market is affected by a multitude of variables, and each year is different. Brokers live in this market on a daily basis. They are your guides, making sure that you know the trends in your market and that you are making comparisons that are insightful, and simplifying the industry jargon and nuance.

Here are the most relevant market metrics that will have an impact on your next commercial real estate project:

Net absorption: Think of net absorption as how supply relates to demand. Supply factors include new construction deliveries increasing supply, along with the demolition and redevelopment of older industrial property stock decreasing the supply. Demand factors are related to the increasing and decreasing footprints of the companies that call industrial properties home.

Increasing supply or decreasing demand can cause negative net absorption, whereas decreasing supply or increasing demand can have the opposite effect. Every year, the industrial markets oscillate between negative 200 million and more than 285 million square feet of net absorption. Seeing multiple quarters of positive or negative net absorption can help you identify if there is a larger trend within a market.

Growth rates: In any given year, and within any given North American city, the industrial lease growth rate changes between negative 3.8 percent and more than 6.2 percent on average. Lease rates fluctuate as supply and demand factors change. They can also fluctuate due to changes in capital inflows/outflows, economic shocks, investor confidence, industry structural changes, tax laws, and other legislation. Note: this is an annual change in the market's pricing. You will likely sign a multiple-year-long lease with annual increases. Your lease contract's annual increases and the overall market's annual increases are two separate things. When these two separate increases become wildly out of sync, that is when there can be cause for concern for tenants and landlords alike.

Sales volume: Annual total industrial sales volumes range from $11 billion to $85 billion. To put this into perspective, Orange County usually sees a range of $1 billion to $3 billion in annual industrial sales each year. Knowing your market size and evaluating quarterly sales volume in dollars and in number of transactions is another good method to help spot trends and identify greater market shifts.

Vacancy rates: Vacancy rates can range from 0.06 percent to 10.10 percent, depending on which city you do business in. For example, in the Greater LA Basin, a 5 percent vacancy rate is considered equilibrium, whereas a 1 to 3 percent vacancy rate is considered tight. This is common in most metropolitan industrial markets. Before e-commerce, the market equilibrium vacancy rate was closer to 10 percent. This has led to more creative property sourcing methods by brokers, which we will discuss in Chapter 6, Engage the Market.

Price per square foot: This is not as simple as you might expect. The majority of the country (and the world, for that matter) quotes prices for industrial properties as price per square foot annually. However, many geographic areas have their own quirks. In Southern California and Houston, prices are quoted in monthly terms per square foot. Markets like Seattle separate the office from the warehouse in their rent calculations and quote each rate separately. In Charlotte, you will hear rates quoted on a triple net basis plus TICAM (taxes, insurance, and common area maintenance). In Florida, tenant use tax is a percentage of the rent, which is billed to the landlord and then passed through to the tenant. The bottom line is, you want to make sure you know what is included in the price per square foot that is quoted.

NATIONAL LANDSCAPE

The national landscape is largely affected by geography, incentives, and investments. Inland and ocean waterways, intermodal rails, air cargo hubs, and interstate transportation continue to play outsized roles in where the industrial market grows.

Here are the top twenty industrial real estate markets based upon figures from the *2020 CoStar United States Industrial Inventory Report*. They are broken down by number of buildings, total square feet, and percentage of the total national inventory.

Number	Market	Buildings	Square Feet	Percentage of Total US
1	Chicago, IL	24,467	1,283,525,000	7.6
2	Dallas-Fort Worth, TX	22,455	968,031,000	5.7
3	Los Angeles, CA	35,099	935,936,000	5.5
4	New York, NY	23,586	826,523,000	4.9
5	Atlanta, GA	16,187	734,380,000	4.4
6	Inland Empire, CA	13,609	664,371,000	3.9
7	Houston, TX	21,335	664,347,000	3.9
8	Detroit, MI	17,336	592,414,000	3.5
9	Philadelphia, PA	13,759	549,338,000	3.3
10	Phoenix, AZ	11,032	358,608,000	2.1
11	Cleveland, OH	8,964	348,971,000	2.1
12	Boston, MA	9,370	344,936,000	2.0
13	Indianapolis, IN	6,595	339,044,000	2.0
14	Charlotte, NC	8,010	334,415,000	2.0
15	Cincinnati, OH	6,954	332,239,000	2.0
16	Seattle, WA	8555	329,260,000	2.0
17	St. Louis, MO	7,302	312,570,000	1.9
18	Kansas City, MO	7,262	311,325,000	1.8
19	Columbus, OH	5,545	306,087,000	1.8
20	Orange County, CA	12,598	300,435,000	1.8

2019 National Industrial Inventory by Market

Looking at the numbers, you will see that the Greater LA area (which includes Los Angeles, the Inland Empire, and Orange County) makes up one of the largest real estate markets in the country, totaling approximately 11.2 percent of the national inventory. That is 1.9 billion square feet. This market is home of the two largest ports, and is the central market for inbound and outbound cargo to and from Asia. I point this out because this is the market in which I have the most experience.

It should come as no surprise that the largest industrial markets are also the ones experiencing the most sustained growth. New construction in 2019 totaled roughly 258 million square feet. When you look at the data below for new construction, you see that we are building larger warehouses, as the size of new warehouses being developed is two to ten times the size of the average existing inventory.

The population density in each market has an influence on what can be developed. Each market also develops differently based on its shifting population centers, new supply chain nodes, and changing labor dynamics.

Number	Market	Average Existing Building Square Footage	Number of Buildings under Construction in 2020	Average Size of Buildings under Construction
1	Chicago, IL	52,459	65	277,846
2	Dallas-Fort Worth, TX	43,110	145	209,092
3	Los Angeles, CA	26,666	43	100,659
4	New York, NY	35,043	44	273,229
5	Atlanta, GA	45,369	65	309,024
6	Inland Empire, CA	48,819	143	150,374
7	Houston, TX	31,139	164	114,057
8	Detroit, MI	34,172	39	143,759
9	Philadelphia, PA	39,926	28	310,742
10	Phoenix, AZ	32,506	62	216,231
11	Cleveland, OH	38,930	7	183,543
12	Boston, MA	36,813	22	91,188
13	Indianapolis, IN	51,409	25	418,662
14	Charlotte, NC	41,750	37	129,222
15	Cincinnati, OH	47,777	13	544,623
16	Seattle, WA	38,387	23	143,703
17	St. Louis, MO	42,806	18	138,909
18	Kansas City, MO	42,870	23	300,898
19	Columbus, OH	55,201	30	325,120
20	Orange County, CA	23,848	16	51,565

2019 Construction Growth by Market

The cost of space can be two to three times greater in any given major market. As you can see in the next chart of market rent growth in the top twenty markets, it costs half as much to rent in Dallas, Atlanta, and Houston as it does in Los Angeles, Seattle, and Boston.

Number	Market	Market Rent per Square Foot per Month	Twelve-Month Market Rent Growth	Quarter to Date Annualized Market Rent Growth
1	Chicago, IL	$0.61	4.1%	0.0%
2	Dallas-Fort Worth, TX	$0.56	4.1%	-1.2%
3	Los Angeles, CA	$1.13	3.4%	-1.2%
4	New York, NY	$1.20	4.4%	0.9%
5	Atlanta, GA	$0.52	6.7%	5.2%
6	Inland Empire, CA	$0.75	4.2%	-3.4%
7	Houston, TX	$0.62	0.0%	-3.7%
8	Detroit, MI	$0.59	5.8%	3.2%
9	Philadelphia, PA	$0.60	3.7%	-0.2%
10	Phoenix, AZ	$0.71	5.8%	4.7%
11	Cleveland, OH	$0.42	3.0%	-1.1%
12	Boston, MA	$0.98	6.4%	-2.3%
13	Indianapolis, IN	$0.49	5.0%	2.3%
14	Charlotte, NC	$0.52	4.8%	0.9%
15	Cincinnati, OH	$0.44	3.6%	-3.6
16	Seattle, WA	$0.96	6.3%	-1.0%
17	St. Louis, MO	$0.46	1.8%	0.0%
18	Kansas City, MO	$0.46	2.7%	7.6%
19	Columbus, OH	$0.44	2.8%	-3.9
20	Orange County, CA	$1.19	4.1%	-2.5%

2019 Market Rent Growth by Market

LOOKING FORWARD

Now that we have looked at the overall size of the US industrial market, I want to show you the major forces that are shaping its future.

E-COMMERCE

Customers now largely buy products online instead of buying them in stores. As a result, e-commerce has marked a structural shift in the industrial real estate arena. It is large enough to have a material effect on the entire industrial market, and its future growth prospects are robust. According to the US Department of Commerce, e-commerce accounted for about one-sixth of the total $3.7 trillion in retail sales in 2019. Online sales grew from 6 percent in 2010 to 16 percent in 2019. In a recent research report titled *Accelerated Retail Evolution Could Bolster Demand for Well-Located Logistics Space*, Prologis estimates e-commerce sales will increase upward of 27 percent by 2024. This shift to online purchasing comes with a corresponding change in how products move from store to customer, which is where the industrial real estate market enters the picture.

The primary effect of e-commerce on the commercial real estate world is that far less retail space is needed in exchange for larger industrial footprints. Recent research suggests that 125 million square feet of distribution space is required for each $1 billion increase in e-commerce sales. Prologis, one of the largest industrial landlords globally, issued a research report suggesting that three times the amount of industrial property is needed for every square foot of traditional retail. Ashfaque Chowdhury, president of supply chain, Americas and Asia Pacific at XPO Logistics, commented on the conversion from retail to e-commerce. He noted that e-commerce takes three times the warehouse space and demands three times the work.

E-commerce can be broken down into three activity segments: omnichannel, Last Mile, and reverse logistics.

OMNICHANNEL

Omnichannel is the industry term used to describe retailers who have both brick-and-mortar stores and an e-commerce channel. Customers can buy in person or online and have product shipped to their house, the store, or another third-party location of their convenience.

As a result of consumer preference for omnichannel, buyers have higher expectations and increased spending habits, and there is more brand loyalty. Nordstrom is an excellent example of this, as they used to be in every high-end mall in the United States. They have not evaporated from the retail environment—they have changed how they do business and supplement their retail stores with online shopping. In Southern California, Nordstrom leased 1 million square feet in the Inland Empire alone for e-commerce fulfillment. If you order clothing online and it is not available anywhere else, Nordstrom will ship it to a store for customer pickup. Nordstrom uses this as an opportunity to continue to provide concierge service: customers can pull into the mall's parking lot, and a Nordstrom associate will hand-deliver their clothing.

This shift in customer buying behavior has led to a shift in size, location, and orientation of retail stores, as well as corresponding retailer distribution and fulfillment centers.

In an interview with Melinda McLaughlin, head of research for Prologis, she explains that not only has omnichannel fulfillment led distributors to locate warehouses closer to customers, but it has also led distributors to focus on replenishing retail stores at a more rapid rate. This allows retailers to provide customers with the opportunity to buy online and pick up curbside.

LAST MILE FULFILLMENT

We will discuss the last place that a product sold online inhabits before the delivery driver drives the "Last Mile" to the customer's house, store, or place of business. Last Mile warehouses are also called urban fulfillment, micro fulfillment, and final mile facilities. This last point of departure is the bridge between the distribution center and the customer. Most companies struggle delivering goods the Last Mile because deliveries are no longer going to retail stores but to residential neighborhoods. Companies are now leasing Last Mile warehouses that allow manufacturers and distributors to hold specific levels of inventory in select urban and suburban centers so they can increase delivery speed to the customer. The pioneer in this space is, of course, Amazon, where they guarantee two-day delivery of products bought through their platform for an annual subscription costing $119.

With Last Mile warehouses, same-day delivery is now possible for many retailers. These warehouses can be far smaller than general fulfillment centers, sometimes as small as 30,000 square feet. The challenge with smaller warehouses is that they can often have lower warehouse clearances and inadequate loading. Last Mile warehouses will usually accommodate parcels instead of pallets, see higher velocity, and sometimes handle returns within five to eight miles of the population centers they serve.

Ashfaque Chowdhury of XPO Logistics explains that the increasing market size of Last Mile delivery for delivery of heavy goods is occurring due to changes in consumer online purchasing behavior and habits. Heavy goods and white-glove delivery are specialized skillsets that separate XPO Logistics from most other companies that handle deliveries in-house.

REVERSE LOGISTICS

E-commerce has dramatically changed the process of returning goods that are the wrong fit, wrong color, damaged, or not what was expected by the customer. As e-commerce grows and the total number of overall product returns increases, so will the emphasis on optimizing reverse logistics.

The larger a company's operation, the larger their reverse logistics operation, until you reach the most massive scale, where companies dedicate entire facilities to reverse logistics. In fact, there are entire supply chain consulting practices that focus solely on reverse logistics. You can imagine how many returns go through a 2-million-square-foot Amazon fulfillment center in Southern California, and that is just one of their 175 fulfillment centers all over the world.

According to the retail analytics firm the Retail Equation, the return rate for the retail industry in the United States and Canada currently averages 8 percent of total sales. Research shows that customers are three times more likely to return products they purchase online versus ones they purchase in person at a retail store. As a result, e-commerce businesses need 20 percent more space to manage reverse logistics compared to retail stores.

THIRD-PARTY LOGISTICS

If e-commerce is "what" is expanding during the current evolution of the industrial real estate market, third-party logistics companies (3PLs) would be the "who." When you think of a company like Nordstrom pivoting from selling clothing at their flagship store in the Fashion Island mall in Newport Beach, California, and all of their retail stores throughout the country to also selling clothing online, you realize it takes time to build this capability. 3PLs companies, on the other hand, are specialists in shipping, transportation, supply chain, logistics, and warehousing. You can see why it would be easier for a retailer to begin their e-commerce journey by leveraging 3PLs' capabilities along with their information technology systems. E-commerce and 3PLs companies in many markets now represent over 50 percent of all demand for bulk industrial properties over 100,000 square feet.

With the rise of e-commerce, the flow of capital going into the 3PLs industry has increased dramatically, causing the 3PLs space to expand, consolidate, and grow yet again. Robust 3PLs offerings are now available on a global scale and can be contracted to provide services for any aspect of your business operations from a supply chain perspective. The purpose of me mentioning 3PLs is not purely for you to be aware of their services. It is also so you can understand they are often a model for optimal warehouse operations, and they are the largest tenant industry within the industrial real estate market. The ramifications of e-commerce that we will discuss in a moment apply equally to 3PLs.

WAREHOUSE AUTOMATION AND ROBOTICS

The rise of warehouse automation and robotics is the last of the main influences within the greater industrial real estate market. Warehousing automation is a broad category with applications in manufacturing, production, storage, distribution, and fulfillment businesses. When you speak with equipment manufacturers, process engineers, integrators, and end users, you really get the sense that warehouse automation and robotics technology is accelerating at lightning speed with new solutions and implementation options.

For manufacturing, warehouse automation is viewed as the means to increase domestic manufacturing. The idea is that fully automated and robot-assisted production lines will augment labor, allowing manufacturers to manage new production methods locally and abroad in a more efficient and productive manner.

On the distribution and fulfillment front, warehouse automation increasingly includes:

- Automated storage and retrieval systems
- Automated conveyor systems
- Autonomous guided vehicles
- Autonomous mobile robots

Automation and robotics are the physical manifestation of technology within warehouse facilities. This technology, however, is only as good as the software and cloud services that power it and that integrate into a business's ERP, transportation, and warehouse management systems.

The constant need to produce gains in efficiency and productivity and the ever-expanding need to meet customer service levels are the main factors that will lead to increasing warehouse automation. The decision used to be based on whether or not you could justify the return on investment (ROI) in a satisfactory time frame. Today, the decision to implement warehouse automation and robotics is a necessary evolutionary step in order to survive and thrive during the next business cycle.

With the rise of warehouse automation and robotics comes the rise of predictive analytics and artificial intelligence (AI). XPO Logistics' Ashfaque Chowdhury explains, "For the first time, we have large-scale robotics that are entering warehouses. There are facilities where you have hundreds of robots and ==collaborative robots—or cobots==—that work alongside employees to help improve productivity. You have predictive analytics and AI technology becoming more capable at forecasting, and the ability to manage on a predictive basis is far more accurate than before."

WHAT DOES THIS MEAN TO YOU?

What if your company is not involved in e-commerce? What if you run a diagnostic laboratory, an aerospace manufacturing company, or a construction company? Countless businesses do not sell anything online. They do not ship products to stores or houses, and they never will.

However, all companies will feel the effects of the increase in industrial demand, due to increasing competition for all suitable warehouses and a corresponding increase in lease rates. During each year of the last economic expansion, lease rates have increased an average of 7 to 10 percent per year.

Another entrant to the industrial real estate market, along with e-commerce companies, is the institutional investor. Due to their ever-increasing interest in industrial real estate and continued pursuit of risk-adjusted returns, the new adage of the modern industrial era is that there are too many dollars chasing too few deals.

One significant implication of the influx of the institutional investment community is the increased investment demand driving down the rate of return for the rest of the investment community. If that were the only significant implication, then companies utilizing industrial buildings for their businesses would be mostly unaffected. However, the increase in investment appetite coupled with the lack of suitable inventory for institutional investors has led to those investors being willing to buy smaller and smaller buildings in which to place capital. The result of this refocusing of asset size is that it is now harder for businesses to buy their industrial facilities, as would-be owners are competing with institutional investors for the same building. We call this the *owner/user market*, as companies can own the building and use it for their business. Currently, the market is roughly 50 percent institutional investment sales and 50 percent owner/user sales by dollar volume.

Although institutional investment means there are more dollars chasing fewer deals, the upside is that there is more capital building new state-of-the-art facilities, more value-add projects where investors contribute significant capital into improving and renovating older properties, and more investment in the software and technology needed to manage such investments.

PROMINENT TENANTS AND END USERS
AMAZON

This book would have a gaping blind spot if we did not elaborate on Amazon's presence and impact on the industrial real estate marketplace. They are number two on the Fortune 500, second only to Walmart. When this book hits the shelves, it will likely be sold on their digital marketplace platform and printed within one of their warehouses. It will be sent through their fulfillment center and delivered to your door from their truck. If you are listening to the audiobook, it is likely on their audio platform, and you are listening with headphones you purchased through their marketplace.

The Properties section of Amazon's *2019 Securities and Exchange Commission (SEC) 10-K* report illustrates their real estate portfolio, which, in North America, consists of 18 million square feet of office space, 20 million square feet of retail stores, and 187 million square feet of industrial property.

According to Bloomberg, as of this writing, Amazon reported its intent to open one thousand warehouses in suburbs and cities across the United States in a quest for faster shipments and increased proximity to customers. In addition, Amazon is expected to increase its fulfillment center square footage by 50 percent in 2020. If the US industrial market development pipeline averages some 200 million square feet of new industrial space annually, you can see why it would be increasingly attractive for institutional investors to fund more inventory over the course of the next couple of years. This is with e-commerce representing only 14 to 16 percent of all retail purchases.

In California alone, Amazon maintains approximately twenty-five fulfillment centers, many of which are in excess of 1 million square feet individually. Amazon is a great example of all the evolutionary factors of industry discussed above, as they are one of the most sophisticated e-commerce operators. A simple walk-through of their fulfillment centers provides you with a mind-blowing lesson in sophisticated technology and warehouse automation systems. If you are expanding within Class A industrial space of more than 300,000 square feet in any of the major metropolitan markets, there is an excellent chance they are in the market with you.

XPO LOGISTICS

XPO Logistics has risen to prominence over the past decade

to become a global leader in the logistics space. XPO ranks number 196 on the overall Fortune 500 rankings for 2020, and is the number-one-ranked transportation and logistics firm on that list. XPO is also one of the top five industrial tenants in the United States. XPO demonstrates all of the admirable qualities businesses can aspire to attain as it continues to build its warehouse capabilities.

XPO uses advanced automation and intelligent machines, including robots, cobots, and the systems described in the Warehouse Automation and Robotics section. The payoff of sustained capital investment in advanced automation creates efficiencies in sorting, picking, and packing. Advanced automation increases speed, lowers risk, and satisfies customer expectations.

Information technology (IT) systems is another area where XPO excels over traditional companies that handle their own logistics and fulfillment. XPO has created IT infrastructure that can integrate with its warehouse automation systems to manage orders, provide visibility of fulfillment flows, and integrate into ERP systems. These technologies allow XPO to enhance safety, increase productivity, reduce errors, and help employees manage large volumes during peak.

XPO also offers XPO Direct, a network of shared-space distribution facilities that provides customers with a fluid way to position inventory close to their customers on demand. There is also XPO Smart, a service that manages labor costs for customers by organizing shift schedules and moving inventory closer to fulfillment sites.

PROMINENT LANDLORDS AND INVESTORS

Industrial landlords take many different forms. The leading players in this space are public companies, private equity funds, pension fund advisors, insurance funds, and real estate investment trusts (REITs). In this book, we will focus on the most significant two current players in the industrial investment space, Prologis and Blackstone. If you have not dealt with either company yet, you likely will soon. Both have aggressively grown their portfolios to the extent that they have reached virtually every market across the United States, as well as having established a sizable international presence.

While the US portfolio size for these two investors is similar in size and scope, they are two very different companies. We can gain context and insight by comparing and contrasting the two, as your company's warehouse landlord is likely to have similar attributes. It cannot be overstated that understanding your landlord will help you with your next commercial real estate project.

PROLOGIS

Prologis is a public company and REIT focused exclusively on industrial real estate and, more specifically, logistics real estate. Over the past thirty years, Prologis has become the world's leading industrial real estate company. With a focus on high-barrier, high-growth markets, they have built a portfolio of over forty-six hundred buildings in nineteen countries across the world. Today, their US portfolio exceeds 964 million square feet. To put that into context, if you took their entire portfolio and included it in the above referenced matrix of the US industrial market, Prologis would rank second only to the entire Chicagoland industrial market in terms of total square footage.

The company, in its current composition, was formed in 2011 with a "merger of equals" between Prologis and AMB, making it the most significant industrial real estate investor globally. Prologis has continued to grow by acquiring the following:

- Keystone Industrial Trust in 2004 for $1.5 billion
- Catellus in 2005 for $5.3 billion
- KTR Capital Partners in 2015 for $5.9 billion
- DCT Industrial Trust in 2018 for $8.5 billion
- Industrial Property Trust in 2020 for $4 billion, adding 236 properties and 28 million square feet
- Liberty Property Trust in 2020 for $13 billion. The Liberty portfolio was comprised of 550 industrial operating properties, totaling 108 million square feet. The acquisition expanded Prologis's presence in target markets such as Lehigh Valley, Chicago, Houston, Central Pennsylvania, New Jersey, and Southern California.

Prologis takes pride in offering their customers and investors the most modern and geographically diverse platform of distribution space in the world. They have over seventeen hundred employees serving more than fifty-five hundred customers, such as Amazon, Home Depot, FedEx, and DHL. Their commitment to sustainable development has placed them at number twenty-six on the Global 100 Most Sustainable Corporations ranking.

Since Prologis is a pure industrial player, they have an unusually high level of commitment to their tenant customers, the brokerage community, and the greater community at large. By "pure player," I mean they do not invest in retail, office, apartments, hospitality, senior living, or any other asset class of real estate. This commitment manifests in several ways:

- Prologis has opened several innovation centers, called Prologis Labs, where they experiment with innovative ways to solve some of the pain points of their customers.
- They invest in startups that work on supply chain and logistical challenges. Customers have an opportunity to participate within this ecosystem and help provide real-time feedback to each startup.
- They continually invest in the upgrading of their properties, whether it be tearing down and redeveloping older properties, increasing trailer storage where appropriate, or reworking property layouts to incorporate more loading docks.

When dealing with Prologis, my sense is that the company wants to accommodate tenants' facility and geographic growth needs. It is often possible for them to expand within their portfolio and to do so in a meaningful way that provides a competitive advantage.

BLACKSTONE

Blackstone's industrial platform operates under the name Link Properties, which was recently created after their $18.7 billion acquisition of GLP properties. As of 2020, this acquisition is the largest private real estate transaction globally of all time. Blackstone has been in and out of the industrial real estate asset classes over the years with their prior industrial platform, operating under the name IndCor.

Link Properties is made up of approximately 250 people across the United States and manages roughly 400 million square feet of industrial property. They focus primarily on major markets and gateway cities, and their portfolio consists of smaller infill buildings, rather than larger distribution and fulfillment centers.

Their portfolio also focuses on multiple smaller, strategically located warehouses close to population centers. This means you are more likely to encounter Blackstone in urban and suburban markets, in spaces that are typically less than 300,000 square feet.

Blackstone is banking on e-commerce growing another two to three times its size and plans to benefit from e-commerce's continued push into infill markets with high barriers to entry. They see location as becoming more critical to e-commerce users over time, and since supply is limited, they see an opportunity to push rents and increase their returns on invested capital.

The increasing scale of Link Properties' portfolio means they have more access to data and tenant relationships than most of their peers. What is more, their operating abilities are exponentially increased within the Blackstone private equity platform, one of the world's most technologically and quantitatively sophisticated private equity investment firms. They invest institutional investors' capital into real estate, private equity, hedge funds, and credit investments, with real estate accounting for $163 billion of their total $571 billion assets under management.

CLOSING

We discussed the size and depth of the entire US industrial market, along with rental rates and future growth prospects of several individual markets. Then we covered the lasting role of e-commerce and how it affects the same market where you do business. Lastly, we introduced the two leading players in the tenant and landlord market, so you can understand who they are and how they operate.

This chapter was part of your orientation into today's industrial real estate world. My hope is that you were able to pick up enough information to understand how your facility fits into the greater market, so you have context as you make decisions. In the next chapter, we will discuss the inception of your next real estate project and how to think about it strategically and tactically.

CHAPTER 2

SITUATIONAL AWARENESS

My new client, the CEO of a national distributor of automotive products, faced a downturn in the market. "We have to downsize to a smaller warehouse," he said. It was a knee-jerk response to what he thought was a straightforward situation. "Not so fast," I said when he hired me.

We had a long conversation in which we went over every detail of his lease agreement. He then discussed the ins and outs of laying out a new warehouse with his VP of operations. We reviewed the market, the vacancy rates, and the outlook for his industry.

In doing so, we realized relocation was not the answer. It was far more economical for this company to find a subtenant for part of their space than it was to move and set up their operation in a totally different spot. In fact, it was $350,000 cheaper. Plus, if the company moved to a smaller space, it would have no flexibility to expand again when the market turned around.

A thorough review of all of these factors led to a solution that cost my client a one-time $18,000 cash outlay but reduced his cash flow lease expense by almost $13,000 per month. This left his company in a position to weather the storm and be ready to grow again when the time was right. All of this occurred because this CEO stepped back, took a review of his operations, and made an educated, strategic decision.

In this chapter, we will lay out the steps that will give you a firm foundation for your commercial real estate decisions. We will discuss how you can review your lease, your property, and your current operations. Then we will discuss how you can assess all of these against the dynamics of the current market. We will not discuss hiring a broker until Chapter 5, but it bears mentioning that seasoned executives usually engage their broker with the inception of a new vision, as their broker will bring insight and raw data to the table. This will help executives size up how a potential real estate project fits into their initial feasibility.

START WITH THE ENTIRE LEASE DOCUMENT

The lease contract is the list of rights and responsibilities the tenant and landlord have during a specific time. Reviewing the lease document will allow you to analyze your company's rights and financial obligations. Unfortunately, getting a copy is sometimes a struggle. The full document might be a compilation of papers that have passed through several caretakers over a number of years. You may have a hard copy in a file cabinet, an electronic copy, or you might have a software system populated with all of the pertinent information. You might have to ask your broker to ask your landlord for a copy, and you would not be the first. Some tenants have me do this without explicitly telling the landlord they have misplaced their documents and do not know all of their own lease details.

What is important is that you review the entire agreement. Check to make sure you have the initial lease, the first, second, and subsequent addendums, and any work letters. Changes are often made in subsequent agreements, such as roof repairs, months of free rent in exchange for extensions, and so forth. Also collect records of large repairs, replacements, and security deposits. You want to make sure you know about everything, especially agreements that might date back to before your time in charge of your company and its real estate. For example, you might be new to the company, and the person who negotiated the original lease may have left years ago. Your old landlord may have sold the building, and your new landlord was not the one who signed that first lease. This ambiguity can create friction and misunderstanding, and you want to avoid both as much as possible.

Recently, I was hired by a landlord to clean up a decades-old real estate mess. She had inherited a handful of industrial buildings in Costa Mesa, California, from her mother. The mother took charge of the property after the death of her father, the original purchaser of the property. Over twenty years, the security deposit had increased, been credited back, and increased again. Then, in a subsequent extension, the security deposit was omitted, and in the last extension it was handwritten illegibly on the contract at an unknown time. What is more, the tenants' records were worse than the landlord's. In the end, we were able to negotiate a good place for both parties and remove the potential for future ambiguity, but the lesson remains. Get your documents in order first.

REVIEW THE LEASE

The goal of reviewing your lease is to have clarity about the remaining obligations for you and your landlord. You also want to know if there are any outstanding credits or debits to your account.

Lease review objectives:

- Double-check the original commencement date.
- Review each lease extension.
- Double-check the rent figures with your accounting records.
- Review the changes made during each extension that modify the original lease document.
- Verify the security deposit amount.
- Confirm the lease expiration date.
- Understand the renewal notice date.
- Read through your options to further extend the lease, and make sure you are aware of the option rental adjustment terms.
- Identify the penalty for remaining in the property after the lease expires in the Holdover section.
- Understand any requirements relative to moving out of your existing space.

Several of my clients have reviewed their leases, only to find their leases started upon substantial completion of their tenant improvements, which occurred years ago. They do not remember what month it was exactly, and the lease does not say. The lease commencement memorandum was not saved in the file, since it was signed four months after the initial lease signing.

After you have reviewed the lease, make a list of outstanding issues and concerns. For example, was there a maintenance request that never resulted in a satisfactory repair? Does the lease state you have to repave the parking lot or replace the roof before you move out?

REVIEW THE PROPERTY'S PHYSICAL CONDITION

Next, assess the physical condition of the property inside and out, top to bottom, front to back. Start with the office and move to the warehouse. Look at the ceiling, walls, and floors in each space. Then walk around the outside of the building. Look at the landscaping, the parking lot, the truck court, the drainage areas, the roof drain spouts, the joints in the tilt-up panel, the dock doors, the dock bumpers, the truck well sump pump, the roll-up doors, and everything else.

Think of this like the moment you pick up your rental car during a summer vacation to Maui. What does the rental car company do? They have you sign off on the condition of the car. They inspect the car by walking around it and making note of any damage. If you do not see any damage then, but you have damage when you return it, it is your damage.

Your property is really just a large rental car! Think about its condition when you first moved into the building. If you cannot remember or you were not there, simply evaluate it as though everything is in good working order right now, because that is the condition the property will need to be in when you return it. Discuss your internal expectations for normal wear and tear with your colleagues.

If you decide you would rather not move, you will use this assessment to help the landlord understand the improvements that are necessary for you to extend your lease.

REVIEW YOUR OPERATIONS

What are your future goals for your company? Talk with your operations and management leaders about how your current operation fits into the existing facility. Your COO, VP of operations, general manager, and facilities managers are great people to start with, and the more feedback you get, the more nuances you will understand.

How do your team members feel about the layout of the office space? What image do they think it portrays to customers? What do they like, and why? What would they do differently if they were to design it from scratch?

You will likely get more feedback than you expect, because every employee will find this discussion relevant. Some office workers might tell you, for instance, that the thermostat is oriented in a way that makes them run cold every day, and they have to bring in space heaters. Others might tell you they feel closed off because of the way the private offices are laid out, or they are lacking natural light. No building is perfect, but it is helpful to hear your team's feedback and understand their needs.

When you turn your focus to the warehouse, you should focus on its flow. Your operational concerns will depend largely on your industry, but you likely need to get materials to the building, bring those materials inside the loading bay, and move them within the warehouse to where these materials are stored. Then those materials are either assembled, consolidated, broken down, picked, refrigerated, tested, sewn, printed on, packaged, or palletized, and then stored again. Finally, these finished products are taken out of the building, put on a truck, and taken to customers. When discussing flow with your team, ask them what is working well for each component of this path and what needs to be improved. Here are some questions that always elicit powerful feedback:

- Where are the bottlenecks or friction points?
- If you had to design the facility all over again, how would you do it?
- If you could have any improvement in this operation, what would be the highest priority?
- What are your current and forecasted operational metrics?

REVIEW THE MARKET

Your broker should provide a brief overview of the market. This is the gut check whereby you can understand how well your initial intentions line up with the realities of the market. If you find there are plenty of properties available that fit your need and budget, you will have the confidence you need to proceed. On the other hand, if you find that your needs will only be satisfied by finding a needle in a haystack, you might want to think about budgeting extra time, looking in a larger geographic area, revising your budget, or renewing and forgoing a relocation at this point in time.

It is likely, at this early stage, that the properties available now will not be the same properties available once you are ready to engage in the market, but this property availability review still provides insight into what the current market environment looks like. By dipping your toe into the market, you will learn what kind of incentives are being negotiated and what the market velocity is.

This completes your first pass of situational awareness. You should have a fresh perspective on your current lease, property, operations, and the market. You will feel more informed and able to think clearly about what to do next.

NEXT STEPS

You have now tracked down all of your lease documents, walked your building, talked with your team, and taken a look at the market. Now, armed with all of the background you need to ensure your success, you can move forward and start planning your company's future.

CHAPTER 3

THINKING STRATEGICALLY

You have reviewed everything about your current property and have a preliminary feel for the dynamics of the market. Now it is time to analyze the results, formulate your strategy, and turn your plan into action steps.

Your biggest question right now may be whether to extend your lease—which most companies end up doing—or move to another building. Let us review the options.

LEASE RENEWAL

Now that you have completed your preliminary assessment, you may feel differently than you did when you began this process. Many executives start off with the knee-jerk reaction to move, much like my auto parts distributor client did in the first chapter. But most of them realize it costs too much to pick up and move everything. Or they decide that moving is not worth the savings of a lower lease rate elsewhere. This is when it is time to negotiate a lease extension, also known as a lease renewal.

Most executives know they need to renew their lease up front.

Their business is status quo, and their facility works fine for their needs. However, I caution you to treat your renewal as a preference and not an absolute direction. Why?

Think about it from your landlord's perspective. If the landlord is certain you are going to stay, or that relocating would be very expensive for you, the landlord will contemplate an increase of your lease rate. There is a limit to what a landlord can charge in the marketplace, but it is safe to say you will pay more than you would if the landlord were unsure of your next move. Once the landlord understands you have options and hears your broker speak about how your company potentially fits into those alternatives, it changes their nature. This is the tactic you want to take to drive home results. You will be more informed when taking this tactic as well.

This strategy can be summed up with the concept of "Always Be the Buyer." The idea here is that instead of actively trying to stay in the building, you actively try to find superior alternatives. It is in the quest for alternatives that you become more articulate about the value of your current lease in the context of the market. This concept is courtesy of Strategic Coach®, the entrepreneurial business coaching program I have been a part of since 2014. If you would like to delve more into this concept, I recommend Dan Sullivan's book *Always Be the Buyer*.

Because of the strategic need to create leverage, you will find that 80 percent of the steps in the process of leasing a new building are relevant to renewing the lease in your existing building. The only difference is that, at the end of the process, you will not have to move. While this strategy will take slightly more time and effort, it will result in a more advantageous new lease contract.

Most business leaders know that commercial real estate brokers list properties for lease and for sale, and find properties for tenants, landlords, and buyers. What most people do not realize is that lease extensions for corporate clients make up the majority of the work for many brokers. These tenant-focused brokers call themselves tenant advisors, or tenant reps. Lease renewals make up half of my own book of business each year. Once an executive has experienced great service from a tenant rep broker, the relationship often becomes long-term.

RELOCATION

Over the life cycle of your business, relocating is inevitable. Ideally, it should happen at the time and place of your choosing. In the story arc of every company, though, there is change. The change may be rooted in customer preferences, offshoring, nearshoring, reshoring, tariffs, pandemics, or in economic, debt, and real estate cycles.

Since relocating is the most complex of situations, we will devote several chapters in this book to clarifying the process. We will go through how to build upon your assessment by adding programming, planning, negotiating, tenant improvements, and relocation management. Each one of these topics is important enough to get a standalone chapter in this book, as the success of each component is integral to the overall success of the project.

First, we will go through the different ways companies begin the relocation process.

SUBLEASING

Subleasing is an integral part of the warehouse leasing business, as business growth often does not coincide with a lease expiration date. This is when subleasing can come into play.

So, why is subleasing so commonplace? If you started your own business, think back to when you were a startup. Remember when you were bootstrapping, trying to win every contract, worried about making payroll, and trying to save every penny possible? Many companies that start in this manner and work through organic growth will look for a sublease property because it is an opportunity to get a below-market lease rate, thanks to the motivation of the prior tenant to move in to their next space. It is also an opportunity to sign up for the shortest lease term possible, in the event your plans change.

For larger companies, subleasing may make sense if you have outgrown your building. Subleasing frees you up to move in to the new, larger facility before the expiration of your lease. When this is the case, executives often wonder about timing: should the company put its space up for sublease first or find its new building first? This can be a complicated question, and one your broker can help answer, because the answer depends largely on the current conditions of your specific market.

On one hand, you do not need to get rid of your old building until you have your new building. On the other hand, subleasing space does not happen overnight; it could take weeks or months. The 2020 COVID-19 pandemic increased the quantity and velocity of the sublease market, as many companies lost customer demand or were restricted from operating and needed to downsize. Others needed to expand, particularly food delivery companies and businesses that manufactured and distributed personal protective equipment, such as masks and face shields.

Subleasing your space can take a while because you have to find the right tenant, negotiate terms, review financials, draft and negotiate a sublease document, gain landlord approval, collect all monies due, receive and review the certificate of insurance, and fully execute all the documents. Subleases have more moving pieces than a regular lease because there are three parties involved: the sublessor (the company that is leasing the building and no longer needs it), the sublessee (the new company that wants to take over the building lease), and the master lessor (the landlord who owns the building).

The initial negotiations are between the sublessor and the sublessee. The sublease contract memorializes this negotiation. The sublease contract, however, does not supersede the original agreement between the sublessor and the master lessor. This means two documents need to be reviewed and approved by all three parties. But what if two parties agree to something that the third party rejects?

Every sublease negotiation involves new variables and nuance. Tenant improvements often play an outsized role. When a company offers their space for sublease, they usually do so with the expectation that whoever subleases the space will take it as is. Executives do not want to invest capital into a tenant improvement project for another company that is going to sublease their space. At best, the sublessor may offer a few months of free rent to offset the sublessee's tenant improvement expenses and then leave the sublessee to spend their own time and effort building out the space.

LEASE TERMINATION

The idea of terminating a lease that you no longer need may seem straightforward. That might be the case if we were talking about an apartment lease you had when you were in college: you could just pay $500 and walk away. However, commercial contracts are much more complex and have much more money at stake. You could have $60,000 per month left on your commitment over the next three years. That means that the landlord would forgo $2,160,000 if they allowed you to terminate.

Termination fees represent the cost of ending your lease early and fluctuate based on supply and demand dynamics, as well as ownerships. Some landlords will work with you because the market works in your favor, whereas others will look for fifty cents on the dollar for every outstanding dollar you have left on your contract—and that might only be if you also find a replacement tenant. Your security deposit usually is not something you can use as a termination fee. If your landlord has an outstanding loan, a lease termination might affect his ability to refinance the property. Additionally, if the landlord contributed toward your tenant improvements, they will want to be repaid at the time of lease termination.

In practice, it is a rare occurrence for a company to sign a long-term lease and obtain the right to terminate within their original lease contract. In most cases, the ability to terminate may be allowed after the initial three to five years, at the cost of three to six months' rent, paid at the time of termination. Any unamortized expenses, the expenses that the landlord paid up front at lease signing, usually need to be paid back as well. For instance, if a ten-year lease is terminated at the end of year five, the tenant would have to pay back 50 percent of the outstanding tenant improvement costs, leasing commission, and expenses, such as demolition, permitting, and signage. All of this can play a big role in your real estate decision.

The termination clause in leases usually spells out how far in advance a tenant must give notice to the landlord. It generally ranges between six and twelve months, but is negotiable, and gives the landlord a reasonable amount of time to market the building and find a replacement tenant.

Landlords rarely consider terminations on leases that are shorter than seven years because of the amount of time, effort, expense, and vacancy that takes place with each lease. Lease-up times can be long enough for older industrial buildings, ultra-specialized buildings, or buildings in tertiary markets where the downtime can be months or years. In addition, the break-even period for many landlords is several months. It can even be up to one or two years in larger deals, due to the significant tenant improvement costs, leasing commissions, and renovation costs involved.

One of my favorite ways to add value for clients is to try and turn a sublease into a lease termination. My perfect-world goal here is to market a client's buildings for sublease and find a new tenant who wants to lease the building for a longer term than my client has left on their original lease, at the same rent or higher. Then, instead of taking on a sublessee, my client and I can take this tenant to the landlord and help the landlord work out a new deal in exchange for terminating my client's lease.

Why would a landlord do this? They do not have to. But if we can provide enough value to the landlord, they may find the opportunity worth the time and effort to sign the new tenant and terminate the lease.

The last thing you want is to sublease your space to a company, only to have that sublessee run into problems and vacate the property. Nobody wants to pay rent for two buildings, and some companies just cannot afford to do it. This potential risk is why turning a sublease into a lease termination is so valuable.

INSTITUTIONAL LANDLORDS

Institutional landlords are becoming increasingly common. If you have one, your broker should contact them if you think you may need to expand. In most cases, your landlord will be happy to hear you are thinking of expanding and will give you the first look at any new building in the portfolio. And if the landlord knows you have a broker, they will know you are aware of all opportunities in the market—not just theirs.

Another benefit to this approach is that your lease expiration date may become flexible because many larger landlords will let you out of your current lease if you sign a new one on a larger building owned by the same company. Also, if you move to another building within your landlord's portfolio, but that new building will not be ready until months after your current lease expires, the landlord can extend your lease at the same rate to bridge the time gap.

I am proud to have worked for two of three generations of a family-operated private food production company in Los Angeles. A few years back, we worked on a five-year extension of their 60,000-square-foot warehouse near the Port of Los Angeles with one of the largest industrial landlords, who is among the most experienced and sophisticated in the country. The client's excellent relationship with this landlord became beneficial when the company considered consolidating this facility with their second 35,000-square-foot warehouse.

After some careful considerations and initial space planning, we figured out the company could consolidate their total of 95,000 square feet into one modern and efficient 80,000-square-foot food production plant. After we shared these plans with our landlord, the landlord provided us with advance notice of several building options that were not on the market yet. At the time, the South Bay market had only 1.2 percent vacancy, so this communication saved months, possibly years, of trying to find the right building.

I recommend doing this only if a broker is involved. While it may seem obvious, it is worth repeating: while your landlord can be a trusted partner, they still have a fiduciary responsibility to their shareholders to charge you the highest rent possible. Your landlord will prevail unless you have a skilled broker working for you, digging up competitive lease comps and creating leverage. While the upside of an institutional landlord is having a portfolio of property to choose from, the downside is that they have more information and experience than you do, and in most cases by an order of magnitude or two. Bringing your broker to the party will level this playing field.

OWNED INDUSTRIAL BUILDINGS

If you own your property and want to move, you need to think through a few additional considerations when it is time to sell. Owners of industrial buildings sometimes have outstanding mortgages, which means they need to sell their existing property in order to buy their next property and will likely need a new loan.

You will want to factor into your analysis the cost of paying off your existing loan and how you will approach your new loan. For example, if your current mortgage is assumable and your loan terms are more favorable than what is available in the marketplace, you might be at an advantage if you can offer your buyer the ability to take over your loan. If your current mortgage is less than three years old, you will probably have a prepayment penalty due upon sale of the property. Check this amount so you can get a feel for how much you will net after expenses.

A few key financing questions to start with are:

- What is your outstanding mortgage amount?
- When does your existing loan mature?
- Is your loan assumable?
- Does your loan have a prepayment penalty, and how much is it?

All of the same preliminary assessment items we have already discussed in the context of renting also apply to owned buildings. However, you will view the findings of these assessments through a different lens. When you sell a property, you will be held accountable by the prospective buyer, not the landlord. Some sellers do renovations in advance of offering their property for sale. For instance, they repair or replace specific building systems that are failing or take care of deferred maintenance. Others take a hands-off approach and price the building in its current condition. Talk to your broker about what will work best for your company.

Most owners are too focused on their company's operations to invest in extensive renovations. There are two primary schools of thought on how to approach property sales:

1. Make sure you deliver everything in proper working order.
2. Offer the property "as is, where is, with all faults."

One would think that "as is" includes having everything in good working order, but that is not true in reality. For example, let us say you operate your business out of a 100,000-square-foot building, which includes 9,000 square feet of office space. After the advent of e-commerce, you shifted your business model to online sales and no longer have a large inside sales team. As a result, you demolished half of that office space to make room for more racking and inventory, and in the process, you removed the HVAC ducting and left the unit on the roof in case you needed it. Now what should you do? Should you have your HVAC guy go up there and see if the unit is working before you sell the building? What if the unit needs a $2,000 repair? What if the unit needs to be replaced, even though you are not using it? Being aware of items like this in advance is helpful.

Now that you have a good idea of the current condition of the property and how you will deliver it to the market, it is time to assess its market value. You might have a recent appraisal from your bank if you have refinanced recently. Reach out to your broker for an "opinion of value." This will include properties currently on the market that directly compete with yours and comparable properties that have recently sold, and may include new developments that will be on the market at the same time as your property.

A high-level broker opinion of value is not a data dump. It should be an executive summary of the valuation, full of insight into how value can be maximized, and include potential disposition strategies.

Most clients calculate their net proceeds using these broker opinions of value, along with "net sheets" from an escrow officer. Net sheets are worksheets that calculate the total proceeds from a prospective property sale minus all of the costs of the sale. Costs can include the payoff of an existing mortgage, title and escrow fees, brokerage fees, security deposits if a tenant is in place, and property tax prorations. Net proceed calculations give you a forecast of how much cash you need to finance your next property.

As a broker, my job is to think about how to position a property for sale. I do this by identifying specific market players that could utilize the property and then positioning the property for maximum positive exposure to those segments. I then provide insights as to how these potential suitors can maximize the utility of that property. Sometimes this takes the form of hypothetical racking layouts, possible truck turning radiuses, or prospective furniture layouts for the office space.

When bringing an industrial property to market, it is crucial to accurately forecast specific demand. For example, a few feet difference in ceiling clearance changes the entire market for an industrial building, as does column spacing, yard size, power, parking, and so on. This property nuance is where the value of an early property assessment pays dividends. However, not all buildings are comparable: in the industrial asset class, each building has 80 percent unique attributes.

Once you know your current mortgage terms, principal balance, condition of the property, and its probable value in the market, it is time to size up your hypothetical purchase amount. We will want to make sure the new property you are looking for exists in today's market and that you can afford to purchase it.

SCENARIO PLANNING

When going through this strategic planning process, it can be helpful to build a quick side-by-side comparison. Each scenario should be specific to the company's objective, and this type of comparison will help you make value judgments and informed decisions.

I work for a global multinational company that is in the infectious disease blood-testing business. This business is capital intensive to set up, operate, and decommission. The company owns the majority of their industrial facilities outside of the United States and had just acquired a new business line, including a leased research and development facility. We had to assemble several different scenarios in California for local and global executives to use for discussion. They had to decide whether to renew the lease on their current facility, or if it was best to lease, buy, or build a facility elsewhere.

We evaluated the markets within the Bay Area, Los Angeles, Orange County, and San Diego. We identified the industry-pioneering research universities within each market and examined which nearby buildings were available for lease or purchase. By comparing each scenario, we realized it made the most sense for the company to operate within Orange County.

Once we decided on Orange County, we could get down to more specific opportunities. We put together pro formas for purchasing land and hiring a general contractor to build a facility. We prepared purchase alternatives, along with general renovation pro formas. Finally, we looked at other leasing alternatives closer to top research facilities. In the end, we decided our existing facility was optimal and renewed the lease for another thirteen years. This demonstrates that only when you come from a place of knowledge can you have the confidence to press ahead.

NEXT STEPS

Now that we have discussed high-level real estate strategies, we can start to translate these strategies into determining what you will need in your next building.

In this next chapter, you will uncover and overcome stumbling blocks before obstacles have the chance to derail your best-laid plans.

CHAPTER 4

REDESIGN YOUR ENVIRONMENT

Environment is the invisible hand that shapes human behavior.
—JAMES CLEAR, *ATOMIC HABITS*

Programming a building is the concept of taking all your operations and growth ambitions and turning them into square footages, layouts, and must-have features. After doing this, you can begin to transpose these figures onto buildings that are available in the market.

Building programming is often confused with space planning. Building programming is the active planning a company goes through to identify what they need in their future building. Space planning, which we will discuss later in the book, happens after you have gone into the market, found a building, and need to figure out how to fit your company's needs into that specific building.

If a company has less than 10,000 square feet of office, they usually do the first round of building programming themselves, along with their broker. Companies with more office space may benefit from having an architect help them, so their team can better identify the right building. Many executives think they need a certain amount of space, only to find that they could have gotten by with less if they had spent a few days planning with an architect.

Below is an evaluation questionnaire I typically go over with clients. While there are generic worksheets for estimating office square footages, I have found the quantity counts that come from these discussions to be most important. Specific size requirements will come later, during talks with architects and when engaging in the market.

OFFICE SPACE
- How many people do you need to accommodate?
- How do you define your company culture?
    - Are there any cultural initiatives or imperatives you would like to enhance through the use of space? There is no better time to institute this effort than when people are moving into a new building. The experience of adjusting to office life within a new space is rife with new connections, new adjacencies, new light, new energy, new places, and new ways for people to work together. A great example of this concept is the LPA architects' corporate headquarters in Irvine, California. It includes an innovative stairwell that goes from the middle of the first floor to their second floor. It is half stairs, half seats, and is used for all-hands meetings in an open and collaborative environment.
- How many break rooms, conference rooms, breakout rooms, training rooms, and bathrooms would be ideal?

- More importantly, what is the nature of each of these rooms? What is the purpose for each meeting room? This concept continues to evolve in building programming. Traditional office build-out changed in the 2000s with the advent of the creative office concept. This change morphed conference rooms into collaborative areas. Private offices gave way to the open office concept to create more opportunities for people to bounce ideas off each other, and to increase density to lower overhead. However, this changed during the COVID-19 crisis, which increased the value of separation, sanitation, and personal space.
- What are the company departments?
  - How many people are in each department?
  - Do these departments need open areas, private offices, or even their own section of the building?
  - Does each department need different furniture?
- What areas need to be adjacent to each other? What areas need to be separated? For instance, logistics operations separate drivers' rooms from customer-facing offices. Professional services businesses separate visitor conference rooms from back-office support.
- What furniture do you currently have that you would like to reuse in the new building?
  - Is it worth trying to reuse old furniture, which can be costly to break down, transport, set up, and supplement? Many companies see the act of relocation as an opportunity to get refurbished, new, or custom furniture. Consider this early on, as furniture can often have the longest lead time.
- Are any specific security or access restrictions needed in particular areas?
- Do any office components need to be near the warehouse or

accessed through the warehouse? Sometimes this is a drivers' break room, assembly area, lab area, quality control, testing, or another area that might need climate control.

WAREHOUSE SPACE

- What is the total amount of warehouse space needed?
  - Break down your warehouse space into its components:
    - Shipping and receiving
    - Raw material storage
    - Low-height pallet stacking areas
    - High-height pallet stacking areas
    - Total racked areas
    - Manufacturing
    - Assembly
    - Packaging
- What building lengths, shapes, and column spacing requirements are optimal for your operation? For example, logistics operations prefer shallow and wide buildings with large speed bays. Moving and storage companies need longer walls for racking and stacking vaults.
- What minimum ceiling height does your operation need?
  - Many warehouse ceilings have different heights at different parts of the warehouse, with the highest part in the middle of the building. The change in height can be two to four feet, depending on the size of the building and the year built.
- What fire sprinkler rating does your operation require?
  - Do you need specific sprinkler head ratings?
  - Does your insurance have any requirements?
  - What is the commodity class of your goods?
- What kind of machinery will you be moving to the new building?

- What are the requirements for breaking down, moving, and installing each piece of equipment?
- Will you add new machinery?
  - Have you ordered that new machinery?
  - What is its estimated delivery date?
- How many pallet positions do you require?
- Will you be using an existing racking system or purchasing a new one?
  - Will you be able to move inventory around during the relocation process? (If you choose to reuse your existing racking, you will need a place to store your inventory while you are relocating the racking.)
- What is your power requirement?
  - How many amps of power will be required?
  - Is three-phase power needed?
  - Is there any specific voltage required?
  - If you need to bring in additional electrical supply from the utility, how long will that take?
  - Will you be looking to incorporate warehouse automation and robotic systems in your warehouse now or in the future? Do you know what electrical service those systems require?
- Do you need any climate-controlled areas?
- What are your warehouse lighting requirements?
  - Has the warehouse lighting already been replaced?
  - Does the local utility have any incentives for making such upgrades?
  - Can the landlord include said upgrades within their leasing concessions?
- How many bathroom stalls do you think you will need? Some workers need their own restrooms attached to the warehouse, particularly those who manufacture, work with raw materials, run laboratory tests, and drive trucks.

DOCK EQUIPMENT/TRUCK COURT/YARD

- Dock-high loading doors
  - How many dock-high loading positions are needed?
  - Are interior or platform dock positions acceptable?
  - Do the docks need to be outfitted with bumpers or with levelers?
  - If your docks need levelers, should they be mechanical or hydraulic?
  - If hydraulic, is any specific weight rating required?
- Grade-level loading doors
  - How many grade-level loading doors are needed?
  - Do you have will-call customers who will need to come to the back of the warehouse to pick up orders and require their own door? Do you need to be sensitive of will-call customers' path of travel overlapping with trucks?
  - Will a ramp be sufficient?
- Truck court
  - How many trucks will be coming to the warehouse daily?
  - What size trucks will be coming to the warehouse daily?
  - Do trucks need to have a separate drive aisle?
  - Is there a need for trailer parking? If so, how many stalls?
- Yard
  - Does the yard need to be fenced and secure, or can it be a common area, shared with other neighboring businesses?
  - Is there a need for outdoor storage?
  - Is there a need for an exterior trash compactor?
  - Is there a need to install a truck scale in the yard?
    - If so, is the scale a platform scale or below ground?
  - Are there any outdoor chemical storage needs?
  - Are there any exterior silos, raw materials, refrigerants, chillers, saltwater tanks, backup generators, or any other

outside improvements that might require additional space considerations, such as footings or screening?

EXTERIOR

- What kind of building image is necessary for customers and team members? How big a consideration is this?
- Are there any considerations in regard to who your neighbors are?
    - What kind of uses cannot be adjacent to yours?
    - Are there any competitors you are concerned about being close to?
    - Do you need to be within a business park environment?

GEOGRAPHY AND TRANSPORTATION

- Where is critical inbound cargo coming from?
- Where are your most vital customers located?
- Where do your most impactful team members live, and what commute times are acceptable?
- What are the ideal cities in your target market or trade area?
- What adjacent cities would you consider if you could not find an opportunity within your target market?
- What traffic patterns are problematic?
- Are there any infrastructure projects scheduled in your target market that might positively or negatively affect your operations?

ZONING

- How does your use fit within your target municipality's zoning code?

- Are there any inconsistencies in your use and the zoning code that can be overcome?
- Are you in need of a conditional use permit (CUP)?
- Are you in need of a CUP consultant to expedite this process?

PARKING

- How many parking spaces do you need for passenger cars?
- How much parking does the city require for your use? (Cities usually require four spaces for every 1,000 square feet of office space, and one space for every 1,000 square feet of warehouse space.)
- How many shifts will you be running?
  - Are there any covenants, conditions, and restrictions that restrict operations during certain parts of the day or night?

LICENSING AND REGULATORY AGENCY APPROVALS

Some industries have specific licensing and regulatory approvals to take into consideration and include within their project timeline. For instance, if you are in the food production business, you know that over the last few decades it has become impossible to supply products to national grocery stores without being certified by the Safe Quality Food Institute. This is the organization in charge of ensuring that food producers adhere to multiple different standards of food safety. I have heard all sorts of stories about how constant Safe Quality Food (SQF) audits cause consternation for executives. It is prudent to know how long it takes to certify your new building.

The life science industry, too, has its own licensing and government regulations when it comes to body fluids, blood samples, and cultures. Manufacturers need to have certain machines calibrated and certified by the Underwriters Laboratories before they can be operated. The same goes for hazardous materials.

All industries should know the process for certifying a new building. If the certification process does not line up with your lease expiration and the start date of your new building, your operation may be unable to operate, or you may be stuck paying rent on two buildings, one of which you pay for to just sit empty. Either outcome is untenable.

BUDGETING

Few things are more commonly unknown in commercial real estate than the actual cost of relocating a facility. You can simplify the process and hire one of the many consultants who budget and relocate for a living. They can estimate your project within 10 percent of the cost, within forty-eight hours of your inquiry. I have seen budgets vary from eight simple categories all the way up to three hundred specific line items.

If you choose to tackle project scope and budget internally, the main lesson is that you need to break your budget up into three components: the cost to lay out and fit out a new building, the cost of the move from the old building to the new, and the cost to decommission and surrender the prior building back to the landlord. For these components, you will need internal inputs and external vendor inputs. Then test your own assumptions and make adjustments. After this part of the process, you can be relatively confident you at least have the right order of magnitude for your budget. For example, will it cost you $10,000, $100,000, or $1 million to move? You will also get a feel for whether or not you need to bring on a project manager to help you further refine your budget and help you execute.

Budgeting is a task that often makes sense to outsource. Michael Shapiro of Relocation Strategies, one of the county's most experienced movers, says that companies often come up with unrealistic numbers when they try to handle moves on their own.

> "We have encountered situations where an employee told management that a move was going to cost $200,000, when in reality, it might have been closer to $80,000. It is all about letting clients leverage our experience to determine a realistic number early in the process. As soon as a company identifies a place or even just has an understanding of what they want to do, we provide them with a budget they can work with.
>
> "Usually what prevents us from getting more specific is just the scope itself. We find that defining scope and roughing out a budget gives clients enough information to know whether or not they should be looking for space. It is not only that we do the homework quickly; we have an organization with over twenty-five years of experience, with literally thousands of moves to draw on. We are not creating the wheel, as a client will be doing this themselves once every seven to ten years. With something as particularly nuanced and detailed as relocation, you are never going to do it right the first time. It is in the building of confidence in your budget that you become empowered to take the next steps."

Once again, the three primary components of a budget are:

1. The cost to lay out and fit out a new building
2. The cost of the move from the old building to the new

3. The cost to decommission and surrender the prior building back to the landlord

NEW FACILITY SETUP COSTS

When thinking through the cost of setting up the new building, you can start with the physical structure and the construction needed to make the building suitable for your company. Some of these improvements will be made at your own cost and expense. The challenge is that you are budgeting without knowing how much the future landlord will contribute for the office build-out. All costs related to your build-out must be considered: soft costs (architectural, engineering, consulting, plan check, permits); hard costs (construction); and tenant vendors (IT, cabling, audiovisual, security, signage, furniture, equipment).

Here is what I can tell you: no landlord will pay for everything you want. The reality is, you will contribute at some point. Landlords will usually provide an allowance to build out basic office and warehouse space with a handful of upgrades. Tenants typically have a wish list that surpasses the landlord's budget, but the landlord will increase the allowance if you can create the right leverage at the right time. Otherwise, landlords who can increase their contribution will require it to be paid back in a lump sum at the start of the lease. Or they will amortize it, meaning you pay it back over time with interest. Your broker will apply their expertise to negotiate the lease terms that best protect you here. This includes how the allowance can be utilized and reimbursed.

The building programming stage is a great time to have an initial conversation with your broker to get a feel for which tenant improvement packages are commonplace in the market. It is also a great time to discuss internally which payment method best fits your company's cash position and capital investment comfort level.

There are some predictable expenses of setting up a new building that will be based on your operational needs. For example, you might need new machines no matter which building you choose. The same goes for racking, furniture, and servers. Bob Barry of John Barry & Associates (JBA) famously says, "Improve while you move." The setup and configuration moments are the times to make capital investment decisions that will pay dividends throughout the future.

MOVING COSTS

The cost of the actual move is one of the more predictable expenses to budget, as the cost will be relative to the size and distance of the move. The main line item in this part of the budget is the moving and storage company. They will ask up front how much work you will do, so they can identify where you need support.

When our company moved, we all packed our own totes and labeled them with stickers that corresponded to our current office and future workspace. We arrived at the new space the following Monday at our work area with our totes, where we unpacked them and set up our own desks. That said, many companies choose to have movers pack and move everything, requiring them to coordinate with internal IT to assist with setup at the new facility.

DECOMMISSION AND RESTORATION COSTS

The other major cost of relocating involves the decommission and surrender of the premises back to the landlord. This is relatively predictable, as the amount and nature of the work to be completed does not materially change based on where you are moving.

Your initial lease review will provide you with insight into the items that are your responsibility for removal. If you have constructed your own tenant improvements, the landlord will usually have the option for you to remove those improvements and restore the building to its former condition.

NEXT STEPS

Now you have taken a first pass at programming for your new building and roughed out a budget. You can now decide what people you have internally to work on this project, and what people you want to bring on to help complement your team. This is one of the more fun parts of the process because you get to learn from top industry talent and discuss how your project can be most successful.

CHAPTER 5

TEAM AND TIMELINE

I spent a lot of time working in teams when I was earning my Master of Business Administration (MBA) degree, and my Master of Real Estate Development (MRED) at the University of Southern California. This was a great shift from the undergraduate days when each assignment was based on individual learning and effort. What I enjoyed most about the program was the breadth of talent in the real estate industry.

What most people know about real estate is limited to residential single-family homes and their neighborhood Realtor. During the MRED program, I learned how expansive the industry really is: I worked with residential condo developers, private equity investors, investment management analysts, financial modeling experts, Member of the Appraisal Institute (MAI), entrepreneurial office developers, family office managers, institutional asset managers, and acquisitions officers. Every project brought a new collaborative environment where we were able to gain insights from each other and work toward a common goal. I now work with many of these people today.

When you are identifying the factors that will have the largest impact on the success of your project, look no further than your team. The quality of your experience will differ dramatically based on each person's experience and performance. In this chapter, we take a look at the importance of building a great team, the different roles needed, and the external players you can call on to collaborate on your project.

BUILD YOUR LIST OF WHOS

Executives of companies that inhabit industrial properties are very capable and sophisticated. They understand corporate finance, operations, law, human resources, and IT. They must also have a working knowledge of logistics and supply chain, commercial real estate, commercial construction, zoning, economic incentives, public utilities, property taxes, common area maintenance (CAM), and more. It is with this knowledge that they can go out and build a first-class team to run their real estate project.

Dan Sullivan of Strategic Coach®, whom I mentioned earlier, puts it best with his insightful concept called "Who Not How." This concept was elaborated on through a recently released book of the same title with Dan's coauthor, Dr. Benjamin Hardy. When it is time to take on a new project, many people procrastinate because they do not know *how* they are going to get it done. Strategic Coach® recommends shifting that thought to *who* will help get it done. This is not just old-school delegation of tasks. Instead, the concept of "Who Not How" shifts this mindset to identifying people who love to do the things you need to have done. This enables you to bring on uniquely qualified, capable team members for each part of the project. When you find external partners who relish the opportunity to work on your project, you create a much more collaborative environment.

INTERNAL CAPABILITIES

Your project champion is the person empowered to make decisions on the company's behalf. For some companies, it is the owner, for others it is the CFO, VP of finance, general manager, or corporate real estate director. The title is not important—what is essential is this person's ability to listen, lead, communicate, and empathize.

Once you have your champion, it is time to assess what capabilities your organization already has, and which ones it will need. Make a list of the people most knowledgeable of the inner workings in your current operation, being mindful that each part of your operation likely has someone with insights and knowledge that you can draw from. For example, from an internal perspective, who has helped the organization buy, sell, or lease industrial property in the past? Who was instrumental in helping move the last time you moved warehouses?

EXTERNAL CAPABILITIES

After you have determined your internal capabilities, you can assess which external partners you need. Here is a list of the most essential ones.

BROKER

Most executives start with a commercial real estate broker, a person responsible for representing their interests in the marketplace. Think of your broker as your quarterback, yourself as the coach, and your team as the other players on the field on offense and defense. You call the shots, but it is your broker who deals directly with the other players in the market. He is the one who introduces you to new members. He is the one ultimately responsible for making forward progress downfield.

Brokers have a fiduciary obligation to serve you with honesty, integrity, and transparency. Their job is to save you time, save you money, and mitigate your risk. Commercial real estate brokers are next to attorneys and accountants in the Rolodex of trusted advisors for any C-level executive. Every few years, executives reach inflection points where they need to make adjustments and capital investments within their businesses. These inflection points usually have facility implications that require the expertise of a broker.

At the most preliminary level, a commercial real estate broker should have knowledge of the local market. You should also expect your broker to be a trusted community member in the market in which you do business, because relationships with other major players instantly raise your firm's credibility within the marketplace.

The second-most-impactful type of expertise expected from a commercial real estate broker is an intimate understanding of your company's operations and finances. This operational knowledge is where the difference in experience and education varies widely from broker to broker. It is possible for a broker to adequately represent your interests with only a cursory understanding of your business, but it is unlikely. The more alignment there is, the better.

The same goes for your company's financials. It is one thing for your broker to know how much you can afford. It is another for your broker to know why your company budget is what it is, because this deeper understanding can help them help *you* in the marketplace. It is common for an executive to stick with one trusted broker throughout their business career when that broker demonstrates a continued interest and knowledge of the company's operations, finances, and the interplay of those two factors in facility decisions.

The third-most-important criterion is execution skills. It is one thing to know the market and to know your business, and it is another to be able to wield those skills in a manner that creates new opportunities and leverage. Creativity is where having a trusted broker can dramatically multiply your capabilities. When your broker has a proven track record, they are able to repeatedly understand an executive's vision, lead a project team, collaborate with internal and external partners, manage expectations, manage market participants, and deliver.

Lastly, in addition to expertise, insight, and execution, clients look to brokers as a trusted conduit through which they can find talented team members for any part of the process. Executives expect these vendors to think ahead and make the decisions that will help the organization continue to prosper and grow.

PROJECT MANAGER

A project manager is the vendor I most often introduce to clients when they have a sizable project. A project manager is someone who runs the day-to-day operations of a project, on an hourly or flat-fee basis. The purpose of hiring a project manager is to have an experienced professional supplement the project team as needed.

On one hand, most executives have competent team members who want to take ownership and can execute. On the other hand, most team members already have a full allotment of projects. Having team members take on a large real estate project in addition to their current duties can sometimes stretch them past their capacity. A project manager has the added benefit of being new to the company, which can be an opportunity for executives to gain an unbiased opinion and create new potential.

What does a project manager do? The short answer is: whatever is needed. Project managers may create the project budget, assess the needs of the company, and manage outside vendors, such as general contractors and furniture vendors. They can work with your own IT department, coordinate orders and deliveries, manage your mover on move-in day, and direct employees in the new facility. What I like most about project managers is that they insist on exceptional performance from all their vendors and will minimize risk for the tenant.

A project manager is also a valuable resource to the broker when negotiating the lease. The project manager can provide valuable input relative to the clauses in the lease and related to construction. This includes substantial completion language, timelines and delays, use and structure of the tenant improvement allowance, and landlord delivery conditions.

For example, in a 100,000-square-foot relocation, you will competitively bid real estate economics and look at multiple different buildings, yet all of the buildings will require different physical characteristics, budgets, and schedules. A project manager can help you build a basic business plan for each building scenario, so you can make an informed decision based on functionality, cost, and schedule.

For instance, Christie Fischetti, a principal at CMPG, one of the most prominent project management firms in Southern California, points out that project management requires an in-house resource with both relevant experience and time to manage the project. "It is rare that a client has an employee with both," Fischetti said. "Compare it to changing the oil in your car. You may have the time, but not the knowledge. Or, you may know how, but you don't have the time. In both cases, it is best to take the car to a specialist who can perform the service with expertise, and for a reasonable fee."

Some project managers can also provide move management services, which cover more than just the move. Christie Fischetti shares that "at CMPG, what we call move management covers seven categories: IT, AV, security, signage, furniture, equipment, and the actual relocation. We can manage all of these categories for a client." Christie continues: "This includes details most companies aren't aware of and have never considered, such as preparing the specifications, identifying qualified vendors, managing a robust RFP process, ensuring vendors meet landlord requirements, overseeing the work, avoiding tenant delays, tracking the schedule, and managing costs."

Is it possible to do all of this without hiring a project manager? Yes, and many companies do not hire one. But why? What I have come to figure out over the last sixteen years is that most companies do not know that such a vendor exists. Once executives become aware of external project managers for hire, they usually give it serious consideration, as project managers can offset their fees with overall cost savings and cost avoidance on most assignments.

If you do not hire an outside project manager, the project champion and the broker will serve as project managers. Just like the adage says, if you do not have an assistant, you are the assistant. Working without an external project manager can yield great results, but it is important to know that you have choices, and you can always bring in a project manager if you feel overly burdened or underprepared. It is worth interviewing at least one project manager at the inception of each project to understand their value and hear considerations you might have overlooked.

ARCHITECT

Once you begin looking at properties, you will inevitably come across opportunities that fit the majority of your needs, but not all of them. Architects can help provide creative designs to a property's shortcomings.

Having a good relationship with an architect, or having a broker who has a good relationship with one, is always a good idea. In industries such as research and development, diagnostics, pharmaceuticals, medical devices, food production, engineering, aerospace, automotive, and defense contractors, we find they have extensive office build-outs in addition to their manufacturing and distribution operations. They will most certainly need an architect.

Most of the time, it is up to the tenant to do their due diligence and decide if the property works for their company. When it comes to office build-out, due diligence is usually at the sole cost and expense of the tenant and the tenant's vendors. It is possible to create a solution, design it, bid it out, and then ask the landlord to pay for it, but this is an outlier outcome. Payment might take the form of a rent credit, progress payments to the contractor, or full reimbursement of payment to the contractor, depending on the job and the market.

That said, some larger landlords own so much property they have an ongoing relationship with an architecture firm for most of their renovations, repositions, and tenant build-outs. These landlords occasionally allow you to use their architect during the negotiating process to "test fit" whether the subject property can work for you, and they will pay for the consultation. The thought here is that a tenant cannot lease a building if they are not confident they can build out the space in a manner that works for their operations, timeline, and budget. This is very common in office leasing, though less so in industrial.

I do a lot of work with architect Liz Hattox of Hattox Design Group, and she explains that a trusted architect can save you money by starting with a block plan, which is a quick and simple fitting of the business to the prospective building in question. As warranted, you can then progress to a preliminary space plan, which has more detail than a block plan. This is where you actually see the rooms with doors, millwork, and workstations.

Liz says, "When a tenant is looking at quite a few buildings, they should consider a block plan, especially if they have to pay for it themselves, because it costs much less money and sometimes can be done just by sitting down for an hour. I find that owners are willing to pay for space plans. It is a normal, typical, and standard practice to see if the tenant is a fit, and they can get a rough order of magnitude on pricing as well. I think a building owner is more apt to pay for a space plan if he does not think a tenant is just shopping, and he's really serious about it."

FURNITURE VENDOR

When you space plan, you must also furniture plan. Knowing the furniture you plan to use will dictate what office dimensions are needed. Knowing what furniture you will be buying will allow you to figure out how much time you need for delivery and installation. Furniture lead times are surprisingly long, so have this conversation early with your architect and project manager, both of whom will have extensive experience working with furniture vendors.

To give an example of long lead times with furniture, when my oldest daughter started first grade, the elementary school teachers were excited about newly purchased and highly reviewed German-designed furniture that was en route to the children's classroom. Its design would divide the room into groups that could rotate through different arrangements. There would be new desks with ergonomic chairs, round tables with low-height stools that could move around and spin as needed, other round tables that would allow for sitting on the ground, and more. However, the furniture did not arrive until thirty days after the school year started. School officials, teachers, and parents had to work overtime and duplicate efforts to move supplies, break down furniture, and move in to a classroom filled with projects, papers, books, supplies, and boxes everywhere. Everything worked out in the end, and students, teachers, and parents alike could see and feel the difference this new furniture had in the classroom. All the other parents said, "Fantastic."

But my thought was, "How could this project delay have been avoided?"

When it comes to furniture, you can reuse what you already have, buy new, buy refurbished, and buy what the prior tenant used if they have excess furniture available. If you buy new furniture, you will need to resell what you already have. Most people are happy to have someone come and haul off their old furniture if they are buying new, rather than selling it for pennies on the dollar. When dealing with old furniture, you have to disassemble it, potentially buy discontinued parts, pay to move it, and then reassemble it in the new building. The value of going through this process is oftentimes offset by the ability to get a great deal on new or refurbished furniture that is delivered to you.

MATERIAL HANDLING

Material handling systems are the backbone of any warehouse. We usually start the conversation by asking how the client prefers to rack and distribute their products. In a perfect world, we then find a building to match their needs. However, we often find the best of the available buildings first, then adapt the client's operations to match the building.

Material handling consultants are the vendors in charge of racking, storage systems, mezzanines, forklifts, conveyor belts, automation, and more. Industrial buildings come in different shapes and sizes, and various systems are designed for different dimensions and use cases. By discussing your upcoming move with material handling vendors early in the process, you can be made aware of any cutting-edge methods and systems that might be available for your new building.

More importantly, these findings may change the very nature of your building search. You may find that your products can now be racked safely in a thirty-two-foot-clearance warehouse, rather than the twenty-four-foot-clearance warehouse you are in now. This may drastically change what you are looking for, where you look, and the type of landlord you will be working with. The calculus changes when you start thinking in cubic feet, unit counts, and pallet positions, as opposed to just square feet. In addition, thirty-two-foot-clearance warehouses also have more modern fire suppression systems and may have more trailer parking for logistics-oriented operators.

You can also think of a material handling consultant like an architect of the warehouse. Instead of designing office layouts, they design warehouse layouts that include machinery, racking, aisles, speed bays, and more. They seek to understand the materials, volumes, flow, and nature of your operation within its current building. Then they educate you on the most current methods of handling similar materials and test-fit possible solutions to achieve your optimal output. These consultants can also lead you to great vendors who can help with supplying fire suppression systems, high-pile permits, racking resale, forklift supply, and dock equipment.

Catalina Material Handling's Freeman Welch starts the process by observing how his clients store their products. "We note their pallet heights and weights, their lift equipment, and the flow of their business. We are there to connect the dots in the warehouse for our client. We assess the lift equipment being used, the aisle width required for the lift, how much storage capacity there is, how high can they go based on the sprinkler system, the commodity and weights, and the typical storage shelf life of a commodity. This is all imperative in coming up with a productive, efficient system for the client."

Welch also uses material handling solutions with his clients' brokers to create alternatives that clients can leverage during their lease renewal negotiations.

When considering a lease, tenants should consider asking the prospective landlord if they have a preferred material handling consultant who can lay out the building and make it a more attractive option. I have found that for certain distribution-oriented facilities, landlords often already have a racking plan they created for marketing the property, and that can save you time and money.

INDUSTRIAL ENGINEERS

Industrial engineers can be powerful guides for companies that are relocating their manufacturing operation, and for those looking to implement warehouse automation and robotics solutions.

By speaking with an industrial engineer about your manufacturing process, you can learn what other industries are doing to increase quality and throughput, and gain knowledge that transcends industry boundaries. The reality of manufacturing is that it is a capital-intensive business. Significant machine upgrades are infrequent. Reorienting a manufacturing process without disrupting client orders is challenging, and space is usually limited. The reality is, the chance to relocate a manufacturing operation might happen only every ten or twenty years. The manufacturing environment has changed over the last twenty years, initially with offshoring to China, then nearshoring to Mexico, and more recently, reshoring to the Midwest. It is helpful to have a guide help you create an adaptable and efficient manufacturing process.

> Bob Barry of JBA says, "One of the areas where we provide the most value for clients is driving home the concept of 'Improve While You Move.' A lot of clients only move a few times during the life of a business. We always encourage them to take a look at new ideas. We share new ideas from automation companies that can lead to a big opportunity to implement these improvements.

We not only help people move efficiently, but we look at a blank sheet of paper to see how we can improve the process with their current equipment and automation.

"We once moved a popcorn manufacturer. They were in nine different buildings, then moved into one. There was a huge cost to do that, but the efficiency of labor space, inventory, and process flow is now outstanding. People who don't move often underestimate the cost of making the move, but they also underestimate the added value and productivity they can enjoy.

"If somebody is thinking about making a move, the earlier we can get in, the better. A lot of people we help move have been in the same building for seven, ten, twenty, or in some cases, over forty years. As a result, they have very little idea of the requirements they must meet now, like ADA or high-pile storage. Whenever possible, we get something going earlier rather than later, because the time can be costly. Time is always one of the main challenges. We have a client right now who really needs to move. They have to be out of their current building in a six- to seven-month window, but with their heavy manufacturing operation, an ideal time frame would have been ten to twelve months."

SUPPLY CHAIN CONSULTANTS

Brian Reed, VP of supply chain optimization at Geodis, an internationally recognized transportation and logistics firm, explains how supply chain optimization studies take the entire supply chain into account when working with clients. He sees his approach to customers as an all-encompassing multistep process that can be either run from top to bottom or just executed at any chosen step. The top-to-bottom approach is more encompassing, but of course is a much larger thing to tackle and can be overwhelming. The following is how an engagement typically flows if you go top to bottom:

Supply chain optimization ->

Supply chain network optimization ->

Logistics/distribution/fulfillment network optimization ->

Warehouse optimization (inside the four walls) ->

Transportation network optimization (carrier-focused strategies and structure)

The main purpose in a supply chain optimization study is to take into account both supply and demand, along with decisions such as make or buy. For products, you need to decide where you should source (raw materials, components, or finished goods in a "buy" scenario), where you should make them, where you should store them (including both static inventory storage and flow points like cross-docks), and how you should distribute. Logistics/distribution optimization focuses on facility placement. A supply chain network optimization study might focus on the high-level business components, like how much you need and generally where, but a logistics network optimization would occur afterward to get down to a specific size and format of facilities for distribution and storage.

Supply chain network optimization studies are the computer models that help you identify optimal locations for new distribution centers. These studies help enhance capacity in existing distribution centers and then help reduce overall supply chain expenses. The consultants study the inbound and outbound volumes of different products, shipping and rail transportation, different ports of entry, and lead times.

Network analysis helps you play out different scenarios to find optimal outcomes in a variety of geographies. These studies will help you understand, for instance, if you can better serve your customers out of four distribution centers in each corner of the United States, or if you should just focus on three locations between the East Coast, West Coast, and Dallas or Chicago. A word of caution with network optimization studies: as the saying goes, "garbage in, garbage out." You will have to spend a lot of time validating and standardizing data to make the study valuable to your company.

A good glimpse into the insights of network optimization comes from Jim Tompkins, CEO of Tompkins International:

> We used to say, "we have a men's store, so the business is going to sell clothes to men." That used to be a good definition, but today we have to ask, "what kind of men? Are they over fifty years old? Are they wealthy, or are they college graduates? Are these people hip? What percent of our market is in major cities versus rural?" All of these factors impact how the stores will work, what the fulfillment centers will look like, and the overall real estate.

Inaccurate and unsubstantiated transportation data, rents, facility costs, and incentives can dramatically change your results. Supply chain consultants like Jim bring critical thinking to the table. They can look at the data and output and tell you whether or not Las Vegas, Reno, Salt Lake City, Phoenix, and Idaho should be considered for your next warehouse in the western United States. Additionally, they can tell you why they should or should not be considered, based on same-day delivery, availability of labor versus rent rate versus productivity, incentives, and suitable warehouse availability.

WAREHOUSE AUTOMATION AND ROBOTICS CONSULTANTS

When it comes to warehouse automation and robotics, you will find there are several different players and terms in this field. There are consultants who design systems. There are companies that provide physical material handling equipment. There are also robotics manufacturers. Lastly, there are warehouse automation integrators. Some providers combine parts of the above-mentioned business segments into their supply chain or material handling practice. All of this can sound confusing at first, but it is well worth educating yourself, as warehouse automation and robotics are no longer seen as some distant innovation. They are becoming widely adopted and are now seen as a necessity if you are to survive and thrive.

In the introduction, we discussed the main types of warehouse automation and robotics:

- Automated storage and retrieval systems
- Automated conveyor systems
- Autonomous guided vehicles (AGVs)
- Autonomous mobile robots (AMRs)

In addition to these, there are older technology solutions, such as picking systems that include voice picking, pick-to-light, and put-to-light systems. Each system utilizes a series of headsets, scanners, and lighting systems to provide warehouse operators with systems to locate the right products and totes in an optimal manner.

Conveyor systems are largely categorized as transportation, accumulation, and sortation systems. Transportation systems utilize gravity, belts, and rollers to manually move products down the line. Accumulation systems, on the other hand, allow products to accumulate where they can, then move through a light and constant driving force. Sortation systems sort through a variety of different mechanisms to move products in specific directions from one conveyor to another.

Autonomous guided vehicles are pallet running systems. They can be semi- and fully automated, depending on the application. They can also provide for the use of a cart that runs underneath pallets, moving them to the speed bay with fewer forklift aisles and automated forklifts in certain applications.

Then you have autonomous mobile robots, offered on a robotics-as-a-service basis. This describes the way in which these robots are priced in the warehouse automation marketplace: as an all-inclusive service. By all-inclusive, I mean you pay per robot, and within the price of each robot is the robot's system design, delivery, training, software, software integration, repair, peak add-on capacity, and software upgrades. The primary challenge for most companies is the up-front capital investment of the system. When this is offered as a service, the large up-front capital commitment is minimized, and it becomes easier to set up a test pilot and scale. The most prevalent type of robotics is found in today's fulfillment centers.

Chris Dozier is the senior manager of warehouse automation for Ryder System, Inc., a leading logistics and transportation company. Chris works on continuous improvement projects for Ryder, whereby he helps the company set up new warehouse automation systems for its customers and improve existing warehouse operations. He places a heavy emphasis on setting a baseline, being crystal clear on the process you are looking to optimize, and working with partners who have a demonstrated track record of success.

Chris emphasizes how Ryder constantly innovates to best grow its value to customers. These innovations lead to utilizing autonomous mobile robots (AMRs) to overcome labor challenges and improve working conditions. "AMRs help team members so they no longer have to walk through the warehouse aisles with carts and scanners, and can instead have autonomous mobile robots come to them. This allows team members to quarterback which products and parts go within each AMR while reducing travel time. Another example of how Ryder utilizes autonomous guided vehicles is automated forklifts to optimize pallet movement when pallet velocity is over one hundred pallets per hour. These AGVs help with loading, unloading, and internal transfers of pallets." Ryder's supply chain teams have intimate knowledge of customers' starting baselines and can then work through volumes, order profiles, and product profiles to assess potential solutions.

Since the world of warehouse automation and robotics is constantly changing, both in the types of systems available and the abundance of startups, Ryder keeps its finger on the pulse of potential combinations of systems that could work for customers. Because of the constant change and exciting evolution of the industry, Ryder works closely with customers to help them understand the importance of asking solution providers how many installations they have executed and reviewing their track record before proceeding.

Working with warehouse automation and robotics professionals at Ryder can offer companies insight and perspective as to how and when to utilize new technology and automation for optimizing warehouse operations.

THIRD-PARTY LOGISTICS PROVIDERS

When operating at scale, some of my clients start to leverage third-party logistics (3PLs) providers to help with logistics and fulfillment. Inevitably, executives have to decide if it is better to expand their operations to support their business growth or to outsource and leverage other partner platforms. If you are evolving toward e-commerce, leveraging outsourced logistics firms can help you understand key metrics. Do you get a sales increase when you shift to same-day delivery? Do you get greater follow-on orders with same-day delivery? What is the benefit of same-day delivery overall? What is the cost? What does it do to your margins? What IT infrastructure do you need next?

Third-party logistics companies can be of assistance as you run into seasonal fluctuations and structural and temporary market shifts. As Jim Tompkins of Tompkins International explained in our recent interview, his client had two distribution centers: one in the East and one in the Midwest. Those two distribution centers are not adequate to get the client through the holidays, so he helped the client put a plan into action for the necessary people, processes, and technology to double the number of SKUs and provide a 50 percent increase in throughput.

Another example of 3PLs rising to meet the market for transportation and logistics needs occurred during the pandemic of 2020 with XPO Logistics. Ashfaque Chowdhury, president of supply chain, Americas and Asia Pacific, explains how XPO introduced a flex program. The program leveraged its access to more than 30 million square feet within its network of warehouses. This additional warehouse inventory was made available in response to those impacted by the abrupt supply chain shock.

"It was common to hear of containers full of retail goods, apparel, and consumer products received within various ports in the United States that could not be delivered to shuttered retailer locations," says Ashfaque. "We were able to provide space and a platform for customers during a critical time."

Third-party logistics companies come in various sizes and levels of sophistication. They range from small to midsize operators that rely on manual processes and a localized presence, all the way to large global companies like XPO, which has one of the most advanced warehouse operations and IT infrastructures in the modern marketplace.

Much of what you can gain by working with 3PLs like XPO Logistics is their cost structure, speed of execution, flexibility, and expertise. Ashfaque explains, "XPO has an extensive footprint, operating thousands of warehouses globally. We are the fifth-largest industrial tenant globally and have existing relationships with major industrial landlords. These relationships provide greater access to real estate and help us speed up lease negotiations for our customers. In many cases, we can also provide space at a reduced cost."

When it comes to speed of execution, you must realize that XPO Logistics executes roughly sixty building searches per month. This is more than most companies do in their entire existence. This repetition of execution in setting up new warehouses means it has a robust process, seasoned vendors, and pre-negotiated master service agreements, leading to a seamless setup of new facilities for customers.

Ashfaque finds that "XPO's scale also leads to flexibility. We are able to provide multiclient solutions by sharing warehouses through XPO's Direct platform. XPO can also shift obligations with landlords, where it leases a significant volume of warehouses. As a result, it can make space available in every major market." This means a CEO who would ordinarily have to decide which market to locate their 200,000-square-foot distribution center in can split it up into multiple smaller locations closer to the customer and make adjustments in greater frequencies.

Lastly, 3PLs can provide expertise. Much like a broker can provide expertise in having the entire playbook of a transaction at your fingertips, companies like XPO Logistics have entire teams of industrial engineers, facility engineers, real estate specialists, human resources and recruiting, technology experts, procurement teams, safety, and much more. The same goes for IT expertise whereby they optimize labor and inventory. The exponential effects of these complementary skillsets result in superior results for their customers.

SITE SELECTION CONSULTANTS

Didi Caldwell of Global Location Strategies is one of the country's most experienced site selectors in that she has worked globally on large infrastructure, industrial, manufacturing, and distribution assignments for large companies. Site selection consultants are flat-fee-based consultants who work with organizations in a similar vein as brokers and supply chain consultants but have more of a focus on assessing greenfield development and the politics and economics of operating in new geographies.

In an interview with Didi, she explained the benefits of flat-fee-based pricing in that once the scope of work has been agreed to by all parties, it really limits the client's expense exposure while bringing a valued member on to the project team.

There are three main scenarios present when manufacturing and distribution companies reach out to site selection consultants:

1. Underwriting and analyzing expansion into new geographic regions due to capacity constraints
2. Adapting to changing business conditions causing companies to migrate to certain areas over time as labor availability infrastructure and geopolitical risk shift
3. Evaluating redundancy, consolidation, plant closures, and necessary reinvestment during mergers and acquisitions

Site selection is most often focused on greenfield development opportunities in conjunction with labor analytics and economic incentive packages. Site selectors like Didi take client requirements and filter them by geographic regions, taking into account state- and municipal-specific characteristics, through county demographics, and down to the city level. In doing so, they uncover different land opportunities owned by public entities, and in many cases, can contribute that land for the development of a new manufacturing plant or distribution center.

Labor analytics is the study of the labor pool as it relates to your company's operation and the geographic area where you are looking to do business. These studies will help you understand which markets have union or nonunion labor and skilled or unskilled labor, and then analyze the locales' wage rates, hiring packages, access to talent, demographics, and population trends.

When evaluating labor, start high level to get an understanding of each market's attributes. You should assess the following:

1. Labor quality: The concentration of workers in a particular industry or occupation, the number of degrees or certifications awarded on an annual basis, turnover rates, productivity, and so on.
2. Availability: The size of workforce, number of workers with the requisite skills, unemployment rates, and so on.
3. Costs: Wages, benefits, unemployment, insurance, and workers' compensation

Economic incentives are tax breaks companies gain when they move to specific municipalities. Tax breaks are more complicated than they seem. There are several different kinds of incentives. Your site selector will help you understand the different lenses through which you can approach incentives:

1. Cash incentives: These are cash, or cash-equivalent, incentives, such as free land.
2. Infrastructure incentives: These include infrastructure, site improvements, and site prep.
3. Performance-based incentives: These are incentives that are realized as the project develops. As you create jobs and as you invest money, you are able to realize the value of these incentives. A good example is property tax abatements.
4. Nonmonetary incentives: These can be incentives that speed up your project and reduce red tape, like expedited permitting.

An economic-incentive consultant can help you understand where these incentives exist and help you determine whether or not they are worth the savings.

MANAGING VENDORS

Whole books are written about how to interview vendors and structure contracts, so I will not rewrite them here. Rather, I aim to give you a short primer. If you would like to delve deeper, I recommend you pick up *The Vested Outsourcing Manual* by Kate Vitasek.

Most executives and project champions triangulate information from their internal team members and external vendors. This triangulation is natural and allows executives to level up their knowledge with each conversation they have. An all-hands meeting to kick off the project is helpful, as it can be beneficial for every vendor to meet the other project team managers and hear their feedback.

One of my national logistics clients is a great example of this approach in action. This client was in the process of doubling their capacity within Orange County, California. Our initial challenge started with a lack of suitable inventory. In this submarket, the base of the industrial stock was developed in the 1970s and 1980s, when manufacturing was more prevalent. Manufacturing buildings during this time had lower warehouse clearances between sixteen feet and twenty-four feet, large amounts of power, modest parking, and minimal trucking areas meant for smaller trucks. Some manufacturing buildings only came with grade-level loading doors instead of dock-high loading.

In this assignment for my client, we located an older manufacturing building that was being utilized by an aerospace company. The aerospace company was also in the process of being sold to another corporate parent. This logistics client assignment occurred at a point in time when market pricing had been compounding for several years. The cost-prohibitive pricing of new Class A industrial buildings meant we had to focus on Class B buildings. We rationalized that we could operate profitably if we could find a creative solution to utilize this old aerospace manufacturing plant.

During our initial property inspection, we made a note of the building systems, ceiling height, and fire suppression system. Once back at my office, I contacted my material handler, fire sprinkler contractor, and high-pile storage consultant network. Each member came out to inspect the property, report their findings, and suggest solutions. We were able to design a fire sprinkler system upgrade that allowed us to store our products at the very top of the warehouse within a newly designed racking system. The fire authority and city inspectors needed to inspect and approve of this racking and fire suppression system—the fire sprinkler upgrade alone totaled $275,000 for this 100,000-square-foot industrial building.

Because we were able to identify the problem early, we designed a solution. Our next challenge was figuring out how to fit this solution into the context of the negotiation. We would need to figure out a way to structure the lease in a manner where the aerospace company paid for the sprinkler upgrade without paying for it as a cash outlay. My client, on the other hand, was a conservative private company that made capital investments in its businesses regularly. We decided to fund the sprinkler upgrade so we were in control of the vendors and quality, but only if the aerospace company would give us free rent to cover the cost of the upgrade.

The leasing concession meant the aerospace company could get out of their excess real estate without a huge expense. My client would be able to make the building functional and code compliant for the expansion of their operation, and we did not have to pay rent on the building until we had finished the upgrade. Creating a solution out of this older manufacturing facility turned into a competitive advantage for my client.

What started as an initial problem for us turned into an interview with each of the vendors, helping us transform our challenge into an opportunity to make use of an antiquated property. It was in discussing challenges with a few vendors that we were able to really understand the nuance of the problem and create a win-win solution.

CREATE YOUR PRELIMINARY TIMELINE

Now that we have thought through who is going to be on your team, we need to account for how time will impact everybody's ability to complete the project. It is in the layering of everyone's considerations that a project takes shape and you can make informed decisions.

My family has traveled extensively over the years. We try to travel as a whole family whenever we can. This includes my parents, my wife, my sisters, our kids, our in-laws, and so on. We have traveled as a group of ten, up to a group of twenty, to Ireland, Scotland, Italy, Israel, Turkey, China, Japan, and more. There is nothing like planning a trip to a non-English-speaking country with a big group to make you appreciate a good itinerary. You want to know where you need to be each day, when you need to be there, how you are going to get there, who will be included, and the cost. You want to know this well in advance. The more you rely on a guide and a travel agent, the more you can enjoy the vacation.

Once, we were in a Turkish airport, about to fly from the fairy chimneys and hot-air balloons of Cappadocia to the timeless ruins of Ephesus. My brother-in-law's first name was spelled as "Tony" on his passport, but the plane ticket spelled his name "Toni," with an "i" not a "y." At the very last minute, when half the kids were already on the plane and the engines were whirring, the airline staff said they would not let him on the plane because of the spelling discrepancy. I was halfway through the metal detector and had to run back to help him.

We were sweating profusely in the small, non-air-conditioned municipal airport, haggling back and forth, and finally figured out the problem. They agreed to let us pass and make our flight. Looking back at the chaotic environment during the airport experience, I figured out what saved us. The travel itinerary! It had all of our names, locations, schedules, and arrangements all on one document.

That document was just for seventeen people. Now imagine putting a timeline together for hundreds of employees, thousands of pallet positions, hundreds of trucks, and dozens of vendors. This is even more necessary because it helps glue the project together and keep everyone on track.

PROJECT TIMELINE MINDSET

Go into an initial project timeline knowing a portion of it will be an academic exercise. For example, a part of the plan is dependent upon securing the right building. You can prepare for the fact that you will have an executive office that requires furniture, data connections, and artwork. All useful planners love prolific boxer Mike Tyson's quote, "Everyone has a plan until they get punched in the mouth." But I think this quote from General George S. Patton is more relevant: "It is in the act of creating the plan that the real thinking goes into the project, not the adherence to the plan."

Who you have on your team will also dictate your initial timeline. Some team members have never assembled a detailed project timeline before, whereas others are project wizards who obsess over inconsequential details. I find that most executives want to know that their team has thought through, written down, and discussed the details long before taking action.

LEASE EXPIRATION AND HOLDOVER

Your timeline should start with your current lease expiration date. This is the date when your warehouse is no longer yours, and it is now the landlord's. Knowing your lease expiration is the easy part. Thinking through all of the steps that need to take place in order for you to be fully operational in your new building in advance of your lease expiration, but not too far in advance, is the real challenge. It is both an art and a science.

When looking at your lease expiration, you must look at the section labeled Holdover. This is the section that states you are not allowed to stay month-to-month in the building after your lease has expired, and if you do, you will be penalized by paying 125 to 200 percent of your usual rent. The landlord is looking for stability and consistency of cash flow. So is the landlord's lender, if there is debt on the property, and the landlord's investors. The reason for this is that a month-to-month tenant leaves the landlord without ample time to lease up the property again.

You will also want to think through when you will do restoration work, do your final walk-through, sign your final releases, and facilitate the return of your security deposit.

LEASE COMMENCEMENT

We have discussed where you are moving from. Now let us shift to where you are moving to. When you are shopping for a new building, you must think about when it is appropriate to negotiate. For example, if you are one year out from your current lease expiration, are there any buildings available today that you can sign a lease on now that will start in twelve months? The larger the building, the higher the probability that the answer is yes. For example, renewals on 5,000-square-foot warehouses happen three to six months out. Renewals on 75,000 square feet may happen six to twelve months out, and renewals on 300,000 square feet may happen twelve to eighteen months out. Leases on spaces up to 1 million square feet can happen twelve to twenty-four months out, especially when negotiated on ground-up construction.

You benefit by starting the preliminary project timeline process early. The primary reason is that once your broker starts to engage the brokerage and landlord communities, new opportunities will start to percolate. It is in the uncovering of new opportunities that you are able to evaluate these and incorporate them into your timeline.

In my experience of hundreds of real estate transactions, there are only a few that have had enough time to truly benefit from advance forward planning. In conversations with architects, project managers, supply chain consultants, and warehouse automation, literally every single one had a moment when they discussed timeline and how starting early had a great benefit.

BASIC COMPONENTS OF A TIMELINE

The basic components of an industrial transaction differ based upon the nature of the transaction. If you extend the lease on your existing facility, you will have one timeline. If you relocate to a leased facility, you will have a second timeline. If you buy your next facility, you will have a third timeline. If you buy land and build and relocate your next facility, you will have a fourth timeline. Lastly, if you have to sell your current building and then buy a new building to move in to, you will have a fifth timeline. Rather than detail all five scenarios, I will give you an example of the most common timeline for a move.

- Initial assessments—one month
    - Lease review
    - Physical-condition review
    - Operational review
    - Existing landlord review
    - New building programming
    - Budgeting
- Build your team—one month
    - Assess internal capabilities
    - Assess external capabilities
    - Select project champion
    - Interview vendors
    - Select vendors
    - All-hands meeting

- Build your timeline
- Market engagement—two to three months
  - Assembling opportunities
  - Property tours
  - Initial inspections
  - Secondary inspections and bidding
  - Lease proposal negotiations
  - Lease contract negotiations
- Tenant improvements—two to four months
  - Space planning
  - Bidding
  - Work letters
  - Permits
  - Construction
  - Inspection
- Furniture, fixtures, and equipment—two to six months
  - Furniture
  - IT
  - Security
  - Signage
  - Equipment
  - Machinery
  - Racking
- Move day—zero to three months
- Decommissioning—one month

Most executives want to plan as far in advance as they can, but the business cycle does not always allow them to do so. They do not always have clarity on their future revenue, operational bottlenecks, or financial obligations all at the same time. I can empathize. Remember, though, your lease will expire whether you have clarity or not. While you may not have clarity before you devise your preliminary timeline, you will have clarity afterward.

I have seen a wide variety of project timelines, ranging from nonexistent gut checks to fully formed construction-project-planning Gantt chart line items. The more complex the project, the more complex the timeline should be. No project benefits from less foresight. The idea here is to get comfortable with planning.

Task Name	Duration	Start	Finish
Stragetic Planning	**80 Days**	**Mon 2/3/20**	**Fri 5/22/20**
Understand Objectives	4 wks	Mon 2/3/20	Fri 2/28/20
Assess Real Estate Options	8 wk	Mon 3/2/20	Fri 4/24/20
Develop Real Estate Strategy	4 wks	Mon 4/27/20	Fri 5/22/20
Lease Execution	**90 Days**	**Mon 5/25/20**	**Fri 9/25/20**
Identify and Tour Building Candidates	4 wks	Mon 5/25/20	Fri 6/19/20
Select Building	4 wks	Mon 6/22/20	Fri 7/17/20
Execute LOI	2 wks	Mon 7/20/20	Fri 7/31/20
Negotiate Lease	6 wks	Mon 8/3/20	Fri 9/11/20
Execute Lease	2 wks	Mon 9/14/20	Fri 9/25/20
Lease Execution	**15 Days**	**Mon 5/25/20**	**Fri 6/12/20**
Obtain Project Manager Proposals	1 wk	Mon 5/25/20	Fri 5/29/20
Conduct Interviews	1 wk	Mon 6/1/20	Fri 6/5/20
Select Project Manager	1 wk	Mon 6/8/20	Fri 6/12/20
Planning and Design	**105 Days**	**Mon 6/15/20**	**Fri 11/6/20**
Receive Architect Proposals	3 wks	Mon 6/15/20	Fri 7/3/20
Select Architect	2 wks	Mon 7/6/20	Fri 7/17/20
Contract Execution	1 wk	Mon 7/20/20	Fri 7/24/20
Visioning, Programming	3 wks	Mon 7/27/20	Fri 8/14/20
Space Plan	2 wks	Mon 8/17/20	Fri 8/28/20
Schematic Design	2 wks	Mon 8/31/20	Fri 9/11/20
Design Development	3 wks	Mon 9/14/20	Fri 10/2/20
Construction Documents	5 wks	Mon 10/5/20	Fri 11/6/20
Financial	**65 Days**	**Mon 9/14/20**	**Fri 12/11/20**
Prepare Preliminary Budgets	1 wk	Mon 9/14/20	Fri 9/18/20
Prepare Project Budgets	2 wks	Mon 10/5/20	Fri 10/16/20
Prepare Final Budget	2 wks	Mon 11/23/20	Fri 12/4/20
Obtain Client Approval	1 wk	Mon 12/7/20	Fri 12/11/20
Plan Check Process	**40 Days**	**Mon 11/9/20**	**Fri 1/1/21**
Submit for Plan Check	1 Day	Mon 11/9/20	Fri 11/9/20
Plan Check Approval	8 wks	Mon 11/9/20	Fri 1/1/21

TEAM AND TIMELINE · 111

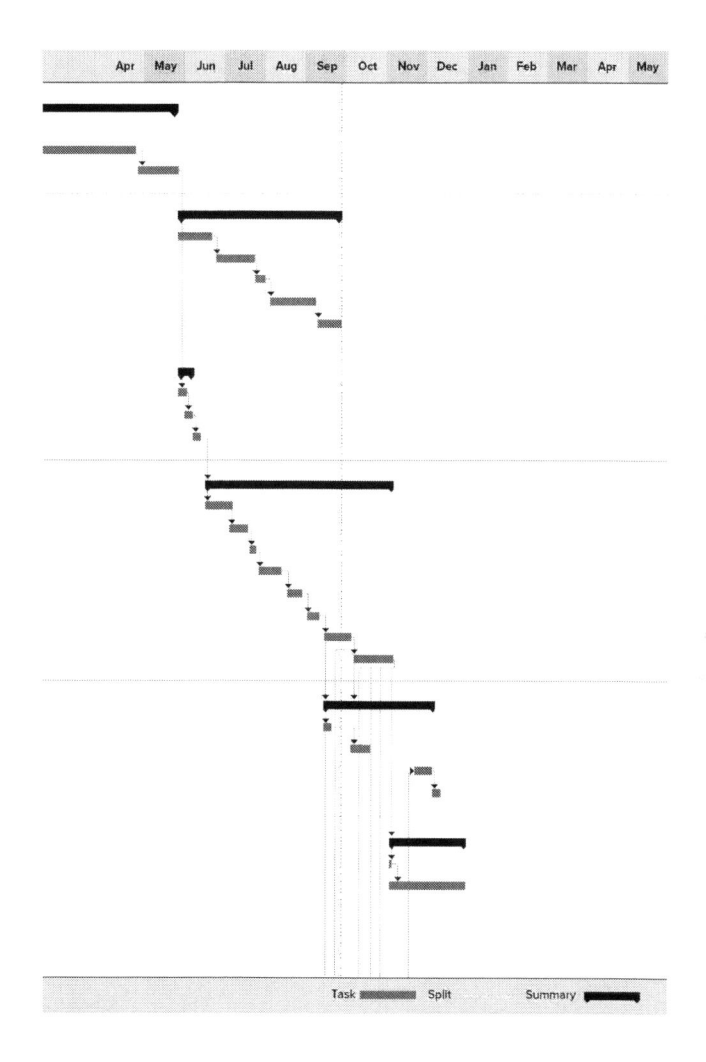

Task Name	Duration	Start	Finish	Jan	Feb	Mar
Bid Process	45 Days	Mon 10/19/20	Fri 12/18/20			
Qualify and Select Bidding Contractors	3 wks	Mon 10/19/20	Fri 11/6/20			
Prepare Bid Package	1 wk	Mon 11/2/20	Fri 11/6/20			
Contractor Bids Prepared	3 wks	Mon 11/9/20	Fri 11/27/20			
Bid Evaluation Completed	1 wk	Mon 11/30/20	Fri 12/4/20			
Contractor Selection	1 wk	Mon 12/7/20	Fri 12/11/20			
Contract Execution	1 wk	Mon 12/14/20	Fri 12/18/20			
Tenant Vendors	155 Days	Mon 9/14/20	Fri 4/16/21			
Furniture	145 Days	Mon 9/28/20	Fri 4/16/21			
Prepare Furniture Concept Plan	1 wk	Mon 9/28/20	Fri 10/2/20			
Develop Furniture Typicals	4 wks	Mon 10/5/20	Fri 10/30/20			
Furniture Vendor Bid Process	4 wks	Mon 11/2/20	Fri 11/27/20			
Furniture Vendor Selection	1 wk	Mon 11/30/20	Fri 12/4/20			
Finalize Furniture Spec and Pricing	4 wks	Mon 12/7/20	Fri 1/1/21			
Submit Deposit and Begin Fabrication	2 wks	Mon 1/4/21	Fri 1/15/21			
Fabrication	12 wks	Mon 1/18/21	Fri 4/9/21			
Shipping	1 wk	Mon 4/12/21	Fri 4/16/21			
IT/Cabling	100 Days	Mon 9/14/20	Fri 1/29/21			
Determine Specifications	3 wks	Mon 9/14/20	Fri 10/2/20			
Include Specs on Construction Documents	2 wks	Mon 10/26/20	Fri 11/6/20			
Order Phone Lines/Circuits	3 mons	Mon 11/9/20	Fri 1/29/21			
Client to Provide Specifications for RFP	3 wks	Mon 10/26/20	Fri 11/13/20			
Qualify and Select Bidding Contractors	2 wks	Mon 10/26/20	Fri 11/6/20			
Prepare Bid Package	1 wk	Mon 11/9/20	Fri 11/13/20			
Contractor Bids Prepared	2 wks	Mon 11/16/20	Fri 11/27/20			
Bid Evaluation Completed	1 wk	Mon 11/30/20	Fri 12/4/20			
Contractor Selection	1 wk	Mon 12/7/20	Fri 12/11/20			
Contract Execution	1 wk	Mon 12/14/20	Fri 12/18/20			
AV	115 Days	Mon 9/14/20	Fri 2/19/21			
Determine Requirements	3 wks	Mon 9/14/20	Fri 10/2/20			
Include Specs on Construction Documents	2 wks	Mon 10/26/20	Fri 11/6/20			
Qualify and Select Bidding Contractors	2 wks	Mon 10/26/20	Fri 11/6/20			
Client to Provide Specifications for RFP	4 wks	Mon 10/26/20	Fri 11/20/20			
Prepare Bid Package	1 wk	Mon 11/23/20	Fri 11/27/20			

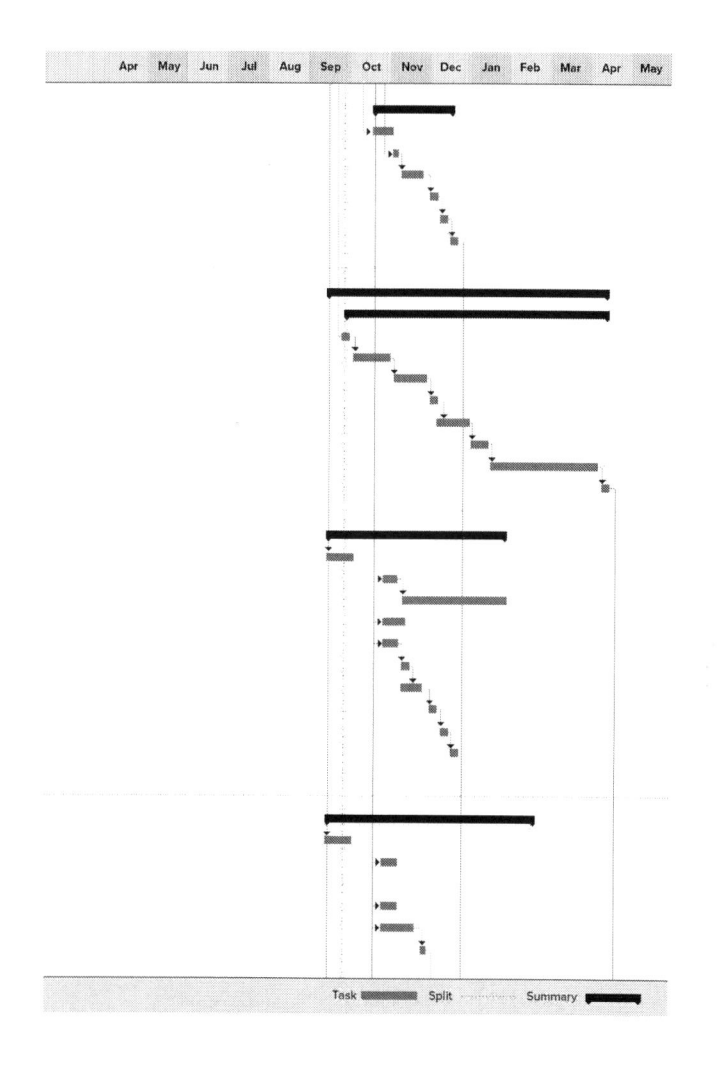

Task Name	Duration	Start	Finish
Contractor Bids Prepared	2 wks	Mon 11/30/20	Fri 12/11/20
Bid Evaluation Completed	1 wk	Mon 12/14/20	Fri 12/18/20
Contractor Selection	3 days	Mon 12/21/20	Fri 12/23/20
Contract Execution	2 days	Thu 12/24/20	Fri 12/25/20
Order Equipment	8 wks	Mon 12/28/20	Fri 2/19/21
Security	**105 Days**	**Mon 9/14/20**	**Fri 2/5/21**
Determine Specifications	4 wks	Mon 9/14/20	Fri 10/9/20
Include Specs on Construction Documents	2 wks	Mon 10/26/20	Fri 11/6/20
Qualify and Select Bidding Contractors	2 wks	Mon 10/26/20	Fri 11/6/20
Prepare Bid Package	3 wks	Mon 11/9/20	Fri 11/27/20
Contractor Bids Prepared	2 wks	Mon 11/30/20	Fri 12/11/20
Bid Evaluation Completed	2 wks	Mon 12/14/20	Fri 12/25/20
Contractor Selection	1 wk	Mon 12/28/20	Fri 1/1/21
Contract Execution	1 wk	Mon 1/4/21	Fri 1/8/21
Order Equipment	4 wks	Mon 1/11/21	Fri 2/5/21
Signage	**110 Days**	**Mon 9/14/20**	**Fri 2/12/21**
Determine Specifications	4 wks	Mon 9/14/20	Fri 10/9/20
Include Specs on Construction Documents	2 wks	Mon 10/26/20	Fri 11/6/20
Qualify and Select Bidding Contractors	2 wks	Mon 11/9/20	Fri 11/20/20
Prepare Bid Package	1 wk	Mon 11/30/20	Fri 12/4/20
Contractor Bids Prepared	1 wk	Mon 12/7/20	Fri 12/11/20
Bid Evaluation Completed	1 wk	Mon 12/14/20	Fri 12/18/20
Contractor Selection	1 wk	Mon 12/21/20	Fri 12/25/20
Contract Execution	1 wk	Mon 12/28/20	Fri 1/1/21
Fabricate Signage	6 wks	Mon 1/4/21	Fri 2/12/21
Construction	**95 Days**	**Mon 12/21/20**	**Fri 4/30/21**
Determine Specifications	1 wk	Mon 12/21/20	Fri 12/25/20
Include Specs on Construction Documents	16 wks	Mon 12/28/20	Fri 4/16/21
Qualify and Select Bidding Contractors	2 wks	Mon 4/19/21	Fri 4/30/21
Move-In	**1 Wk**	**Mon 5/3/21**	**Fri 5/7/21**

TEAM AND TIMELINE · 115

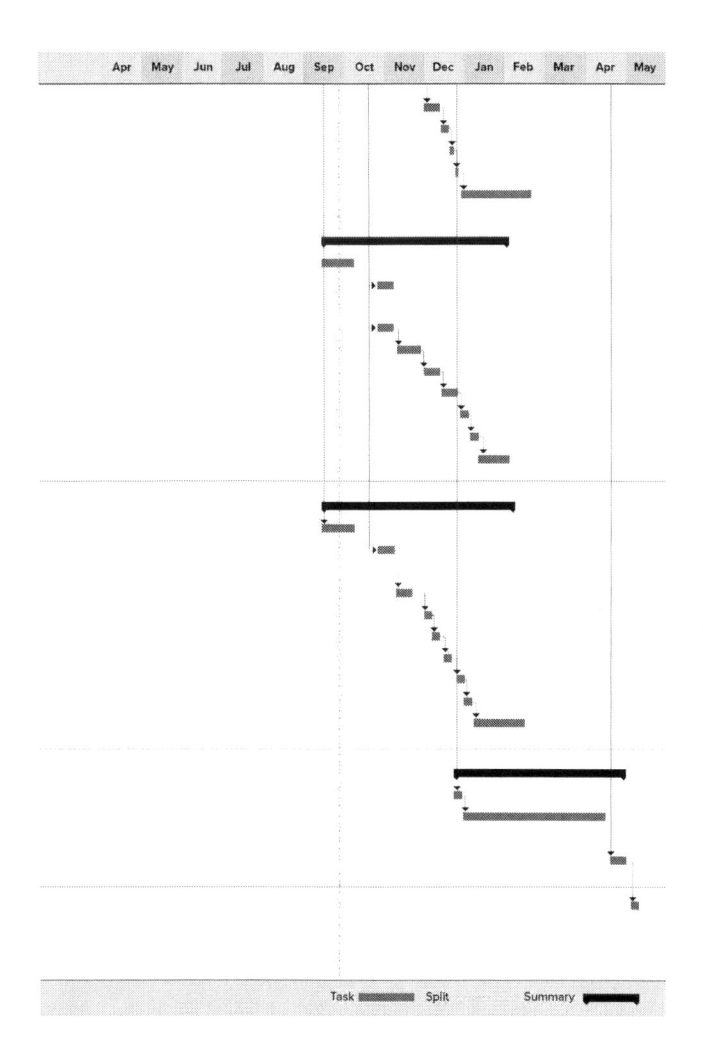

NEXT STEPS

Now it is time to take your timeline into the marketplace and alter it based on real-life conditions. It is helpful to know what buildings are available, as properties are available at specific points in time. You might find the perfect building available now, but you need six months before you can lease it. You might find that a less-than-ideal building is available, but it is available at your ideal time. Can you modify the building to make it a win-win scenario? Only by engaging in the market will you be able to make these kinds of judgment calls.

CHAPTER 6

ENGAGE THE MARKET

Now we are getting to what people generally think of as the "fun" part of commercial real estate: kicking the tires on properties and working on the deal. At times, finding the right building, getting a good deal, and winning an intense negotiation can be fun. Other times, it can become a tough process where finding the right building takes months and getting a good deal means simply getting the best deal you can. Sometimes, winning an intense negotiation results in some loss of goodwill. This chapter will steer you toward a more positive process.

Market engagement is not only important when your lease is up and you want to move—it is also important when you want to renew your lease and stay put. If you want to have leverage in your renewal negotiations, your landlord should know you have actively and intelligently evaluated your business plans and your property needs. My team handles dozens of renewals each year, and we have found that the discovery process of market engagement always leads to new insights, negotiating strategies, and ultimately, landlord concessions.

ASSEMBLE OPPORTUNITIES

When it comes to assembling opportunities, the best brokers find what is available and discover what is off market. We will focus here on looking at the spectrum of effort needed to find the right opportunity, so you understand which approach is appropriate for your situation.

Let us talk about a typical small space. It might require utilizing the basic multiple listing service (MLS), filtering opportunities, prioritizing them, setting up a tour, and selecting a match. It is simple, straightforward, and everybody is happy. These are the experiences people have in mind when they are thinking about doing it themselves. I have found this works when you need less than 2,000 square feet of warehouse with two offices, a restroom, and a roll-up door. When dealing with small spaces, try to keep it simple.

On the other side of the spectrum are the larger, more sophisticated searches you might read about in the news: Tesla's Reno Gigafactory, Amazon's HQ2 property search, or Toyota moving its headquarters from California to Texas. This type of search might require teams of consultants evaluating different factors like labor wages and availability, economic tax incentives, supply chain and logistics of inbound raw materials, outbound finished goods, utility availability and rates, feasibility studies, land site availability, different property developer partners, and more. It can take months to understand feasibility, and years of execution to result in a new plant that is open and operating.

In this book, I am focusing on where most deals take place: the middle ground, in the range of 20,000 to 500,000 square feet. In these situations, finding the right property can have an extraordinary impact on the future success of the company. The property can help or hinder the company's culture, productivity, and efficiency.

One of the primary roles of your broker is finding property opportunities for you. This goes way beyond a quick search of the MLS.

A great broker leverages relationships within the brokerage community to find opportunities that are not yet available. Here are some of the most common ways I do this:

1. Communicate with other brokers who represent landlords and have similar listings. Frequently, these brokers will have long-term relationships with their landlord clients and will know about other spaces coming to market within the next six to twelve months. Because I have built a relationship with each broker over time, they trust me, and they can usually ask questions of their clients to find additional opportunities.
2. Communicate with institutional investors and developers about their rent rolls. It is only through years of working with them that I have found it is possible to find opportunities that are not publicly available. This is about 25 to 30 percent of the market, which companies would not know about otherwise.
3. Speak with the investment community about their acquisitions pipeline. Some investors, both private high-net-worth individuals and large institutions, purchase vacant properties that need tenants. These same investors will buy additional property based on having a known tenant to lease that property. We can sometimes find a property that is for sale and line up a purchase subject to the successful simultaneous negotiation of a lease with our clients. This is called the "tenant in tow" method.

4. Brainstorm with developers who own land sites about their plans to build new industrial buildings. We have found that industrial developers will develop based on speculative building features and characteristics when they do not already have a tenant. When they do have a tenant interested in their land site, they will customize their plans to suit the needs of this prospective tenant. This tailoring of the site, structure, and interior build-out can be a great way to create a win-win solution for clients and developers alike.
5. I market client requirements directly to private property owners through my phone, email, and postcards, utilizing my proprietary property database. This often leads to new opportunities where my clients do not have to compete with the market to win favorable terms.
6. I market my clients' requirements on LinkedIn. I invest and engage far and wide in my LinkedIn social media Rolodex of contacts for this specific reason. I have regularly found new, timely opportunities for my clients by broadcasting our geographic area, size, clearance, and timing to the wider brokerage and investment community.

PROPERTY TOURS

Property tours are fun. Most executives enjoy getting into the marketplace to see, touch, and feel each property to judge how well it matches their vision for their company's future. At a minimum, the broker should vet the industrial property frequently, and the project champion and internal team will vet it as well, before it is worth the executive's time.

Great tours are flexible and adaptable based on real-time feedback. Some properties that seem like a perfect fit end up being dismissed based on small factors. A broker's job is to make the best opportunities available for the executive on a silver platter, so the executive can pick and choose as their vision allows.

In advance of any tour, we prepare a short list of three to five available buildings, prioritized by the overall fit to the client's needs, operationally and financially. Tours usually last one to four hours, including drive time and coffee or lunch as needed.

The circumstances of the tour are different for each building. Some properties may be vacant, and an owner's representative will need to be present. Some properties with existing tenants may require notice before allowing visitors. Some properties will only accommodate tours at specific times, based on the existing tenant's schedule or shift changes. Others may have forklifts, equipment, or machines running while you are in the building. Many have safety protocols for hard hats, face masks, smocks, or staying on a specific path of travel to ensure everybody's safety.

INITIAL INSPECTIONS

When I am touring with clients, I usually take notes of what they like and what they do not like. I then take that analysis back to integrate and reprioritize our list of opportunities to determine future action. I like to inspect properties outside to inside, top to bottom, front to back.

On the outside, you must be able to get through the highways, streets, and driveways to find the building. You need to be able to get to the parking lot and through the access ways to safely reach the entrance. The building image needs to match, or have the ability to match, the company's culture. We often take inventory of the surrounding neighbors, from both an image and a use perspective. You will not be able to change your neighboring business's image, but you can use it to understand the local property zoning and any business park covenants, conditions, and restrictions (CC&Rs) that might restrict specific uses from the project. The zoning and CC&Rs, or lack of CC&Rs, could mean the difference between an unsightly tow yard moving in next to you mid-lease, or a nice, clean corporate neighbor. It is also good to know whether your neighbors have any environmentally hazardous processes that might cause odor, air hazards, or soil or groundwater issues.

On the inside, we usually start with the office and make sure there is enough space for each department and each key personnel. We then look at the construction of the office ceiling grid, height, penetrations, lighting methods, layout efficiency, orientation of restrooms, path of travel, and any Americans with Disabilities Act (ADA) considerations. We usually do not take too much stock of existing flooring, as it is usually slated to be replaced for a new office build-out.

As we pass through the office into the warehouse, we look at the warehouse ceiling height(s). Ceiling height advertisements are not always verified, so it is worth bringing a laser measurer to check where the roof meets the concrete tilt-up panel, and the height in the middle of the warehouse, on the underside of the lowest laminated wood beam. Industrial building roofs with laminated wood beams often bow in different areas of the warehouse.

Fire sprinkler pipes and sprinkler heads will be lower than the roof girders and support beams. The roof height and sprinkler system are essential to determine how high you can rack. Skylights and insulation provide clues as to the roof condition, as both will show signs of active and prior water intrusion. An optimal quantity of skylights can lead to electricity savings by increasing natural light in the warehouse, but skylights are also the weakest part of the roof structure. We ask when the roof and skylights were replaced, to know what kind of risk is involved, and who is responsible for fixing leaks.

It is helpful to look at the condition of the warehouse floor. A concrete slab tells you a story. You will be able to notice where machines used to be located, past water leaks, racking bolt divots, cracks, unsettled panels, expansive soils, signs of environmental testing, and more. Looking at the warehouse floor is like playing "Sherlock Holmes," where you can see into the past by looking at the present condition. This will help you understand what kind of work the foundation may need in order to be suitable for your needs.

This tour is a chance to see how each item on your programming list relates to the physical environment and condition of the present building. This forms the basis for your future inspections, contractor bids, and landlord negotiations. The tour is also a chance to bond with your team and create the right experience for the client so they can make the most of the opportunity.

VENDOR WALK-THROUGHS

Inevitably, you will need to make changes to the property and adjust the project plan to tailor both to the realities of the marketplace. So, after the initial inspection, it is prudent to schedule a second walk-through for the architect, general contractor, internal teams, and external vendors. They will be responsible for creating solutions and providing cost estimates. It is usually best to schedule this for a day when vendors will minimally disrupt any existing tenants.

You will find that a good architect or project manager can save everyone lots of time because they work with general contractors and subcontractors daily and can accurately estimate pricing. Pricing estimates save time when making assumptions and filtering properties during feasibility. We can then further revise our assumptions when we go through the space planning, pricing plan, and general-contractor bidding process.

If there is a high probability you will be renewing your lease, yet you are in the market to ensure you have credible alternatives available to you, this is where you have to use your best judgment as to whether or not it makes sense to bring the vendors back, or to engage in the space-planning process below.

SPACE PLANNING

We think about initial space planning during the tour to help you think through what changes need to be made in order to make the fit optimal.

We start with the reception area, where visitors gain a first impression of your company's brand and culture. Imagine walking in the door and seeing just one small room with a dark-stained wood reception desk, dim lighting, gray commercial-grade carpet, and a sign tacked onto the drywall in the back of the reception area. This is usually what you imagine when you think of a small warehouse unit. Functional but uninspiring.

Now imagine you walk into a space with natural light and an

open feel. Your first step into the space is on polished concrete with a sheen that reflects the circular LED lighting hanging from the rafters above you. You see a reception station that seems to waterfall over the counter's edge, set in front of a wall displaying the company logo.

With a few key design choices up front, it is possible to tie in details to connect your space and your brand, showing visitors their experience is important to you. Consider the conference rooms, the kitchens, and the restrooms.

Conference room tables and seating are always a point of contention between the executive who wants to reuse that old wooden fifteen-foot conference table from the 1970s, and the executive who wants a two-thousand-pound solid marble slab imported from Italy. I joke, but you would be surprised how often people think they need a certain type of conference room, only to create a very large or elaborate one that is used infrequently.

Today's trends in kitchens and copy rooms turn them into open areas that double as cafés and work areas. They are often oriented so they can be open for collaboration without bringing excessive noise into the rest of the office. This means break rooms and copy rooms are no longer dark, dingy, disconnected places.

The best part of tenant improvements is that when they are designed early in the space-planning process and included within the tenant improvement package, the landlord can construct them for you. This is where early and thoughtful engagement within the process can pay dividends.

The deliverables here, in a perfect world, are a floor plan and site plan including all the changes needed, along with an overlay of furniture, racking, and machinery. This drawing may be from an architect, furniture vendor, material handling consultant, industrial engineer, or all four. What is important is that someone has all of these in one place and has thought through their relation to one another.

FIND THE RIGHT COMPETITIVE NEGOTIATION BALANCE

Once you have found the right building, it is time to negotiate terms.

There are limits and balance to negotiating, of course. You will see some "tenant rep only" firms take an overly aggressive tack in this process and string along multiple landlords to the point that each one spends money on their behalf to create plans and carefully craft legal contract documents, which only become leverage. The reps can often take a "win at all costs" mentality and create a lot of dissatisfaction along the way. I am all for maximizing opportunities for clients, but only in a way that is honest and genuine.

Another such balance is between your current and prospective landlord. Rarely is it practical or desirable to need more than three options to create the optimal outcome. How you negotiate will depend on the market dynamic.

When talking to brokers who represent landlords, I gauge their property's activity levels. Some brokers can be intentionally vague about their interest in a given property, thinking this approach gives them a better chance of bringing their client the most opportunities. I have learned to clearly ask landlord brokers if they have any current proposals and make them objectively answer this question. This direct question will allow you to finalize how you prioritize that property.

Each company will have a different tactic when it comes to negotiating on multiple buildings. The rule here is that you should only negotiate on buildings you would sincerely sign a lease on if the terms were favorable. This sincerity can sometimes lead executives to negotiate on just one property in good faith. This is because there is usually a small window of time to identify the perfect fit and secure it without competing.

That said, I work on several negotiations a year where we put out requests for proposals to multiple landlords on multiple buildings, filter and analyze all the responses, and then decide which landlords to engage further. Think of it like the NCAA March Madness tournament where there is a bracket of college basketball teams and each one faces off against others. We all obsessively watch the results until there are two teams remaining that tensely battle back and forth until the last seconds on the clock, resulting in an undisputed winner. Which tactic we take is determined by the market dynamic.

NEXT STEPS

Market engagement is the precursor to lease proposal negotiations, lease contract negotiations, construction, and relocation. It is this market engagement that sets the stage for everything that will materialize in the future. There is a literal translation from what your team sees in the field to what we negotiate in lease proposals. This forms the backbone for the work of the landlord's attorney in drafting the final lease document, which will include the construction drawings and work letter.

This direct relationship between market engagement and future success of the company is the reason why we usually tour the same properties multiple times, with multiple team members. We enjoy having every team member evaluate the property with their unique perspective to ensure that all relevant property-related concerns are addressed within the lease proposal and the ensuing lease contract negotiation. Now it is time to talk about how we structure that lease proposal.

CHAPTER 7

PROPOSALS AND PROJECTIONS

Once you find a building that works for you, you can craft your lease proposal. This precedes the lease contract negotiation. It contains the major business points that need to be agreed upon before the deal goes to a full contract. Sometimes companies will hurriedly forget to include some nuanced items within their proposals, to their detriment. Other companies will negotiate the lease proposal as if it were the lease contract itself and cover extraneous topics that aggravate rather than elevate the conversation. Experienced brokers understand this delicate balance. The two foundational elements of a winning lease proposal are:

1. Thoughtful consideration of how the property matches the company's needs operationally and financially
2. An understanding that the lease needs to work for both parties

In this chapter, we will talk about what goes into a lease proposal. Then we will think through how to analyze the economics.

LEASE PROPOSAL

Let us start with the lease proposal itself. If the proposal is accepted, it will be used by the landlord's attorney to prepare the lease contract. Here is an overview of the universal lease proposal sections:

PARTIES

The parties are the trade names, or official legal entities, for both the landlord and the tenant. It is essential to communicate who will be on the lease so there is no ambiguity: will it be a principal of the company, a newly set up corporation, a subsidiary, or a corporate parent? Landlords want to make sure your financials match the entity, as well as verify the corporate officers in charge of signing the lease.

PROPERTY ADDRESS

This one is self-explanatory. On the odd occasion, we have had to change the property address number, letter, or suite based on client preference. This is surprisingly possible and less difficult than one would expect, provided the United States Postal Service and local fire authority are on board.

PREMISES SIZE

This is the approximate size of the building in question. Some people will get caught up in the exact measurements of the building, but building square footage is always an approximation. If you hired five different architects to measure the building using industry standards, you would likely get five different numbers. You must rely on the fact that the space is adequate for your business operations and that the total amount of square footage is approximate and reasonable. When in doubt, the Building Owners and Managers Association (BOMA) is the primary authority on measuring square footage. Their most current standard of measurement guidelines can be purchased through BOMA and SIOR. When in doubt, ask your architect.

LEASE COMMENCEMENT DATE

This is the crucial date when you will formally take possession of the property and start paying rent. This date is equally important for the landlord, as they have to guarantee completion of any tenant improvements or construction by this date, or they incur penalties. This date is different from early occupancy or free rent.

LEASE TERM

This is the length of time you want to be able to utilize the property. It is customary to have full-year lease terms. While it is customary to lease for full years at a time, do not worry about asking for a specific lease expiration month if it works better for your business and makes for a less disruptive time to move. For example, one of my clients finds it ideal to have all their leases expire on December 31. We have negotiated every single one of their leases to have the same expiration date so we do not interfere with their busiest times of the year. Landlords are usually empathetic and accommodating when it comes to this type of request.

LEASE RATE

The lease rate is quoted per square foot, per month in Southern California, Houston, and a handful of other markets, and per square foot, per year everywhere else. In certain markets, such as Seattle, they quote lease rates differently for the office portion and the warehouse portion of the space. You will always want to know if your lease includes any of the property operating expenses in it. We will cover this in the subsequent section on Lease Type.

LEASE RATE ADJUSTMENTS / ESCALATIONS / ANNUAL INCREASES

This section describes how much rent will increase each year. The general idea is that the base rate should adjust each year to keep up with inflation. In practice, this is subject to supply and demand market dynamics at the time of the negotiation. When I started in this business in 2004, there were still instances where we would negotiate annual rent increases based on the Consumer Price Index, which at the time averaged 2.1 percent. Over the next decade, the industry standard transformed to a uniform 3 percent.

As the market tightened in 2018, we started to see 3 to 4.5 percent annual increases, which had less to do with inflation and more to do with market rent demand. If you were not paying attention and accepted a 4.5 percent increase rather than a 3 percent increase, you would have paid an extra two months of rent over five years that you could have invested in your company instead. In Southern California, the industrial market averaged 7.5 percent market growth in lease rates from 2014 to 2019. Those who signed a five-year lease in 2014 with 3 percent increases received an unpleasant surprise during their subsequent lease negotiation.

LEASE TYPE

The purpose of lease types is to set expectations and give a broad brushstroke as to what to expect, but the specific language buried deep in the lease dictates the real terms. As a result, you can find two leases with identical language but called different types of leases. Therefore, it is essential to come to each lease with a fresh perspective, ready to identify who is responsible for what.

The lease type denotes the inclusion or exclusion of property operating expenses within the lease rate being quoted. Lease types can include industrial gross, gross, modified gross, modified net, single net, double net, triple net, and absolute net. The main leases you will encounter in the market are:

- Gross: This lease rental payment includes payment for rent, property tax, insurance, and common area maintenance expenses. This is typically found with older, privately held landlords.
- Modified gross: This rental payment includes payment for rent, property tax, and insurance, but not common area maintenance.
- Triple net: This lease rental payment only includes rent. Property tax, insurance, and common area maintenance are paid separately. Each "net" within the term "triple net lease" represents an operating expense, namely, property tax, insurance, and common area maintenance. This type of lease is commonly found with institutional landlords and landlords who have purchased property within the last ten years.

Any deviation from this represents a shift of the property tax, insurance, or common area maintenance into the rent or into the operating expenses to be paid separately. This is where your broker and attorney can help you make sure you are very clear on what your responsibilities and expenses are for each type of lease.

At first, understanding lease types can be confusing to non-industry-insiders and less- experienced executives. At the bare minimum for all types of leases, you should be prepared to take care of all interior property maintenance on your own, including HVAC maintenance, doors, windows, ceiling tiles, lights, bathroom fixtures, roll-up doors, and dock bumpers. It pays to have your broker and attorney explain it and look out for you until you firmly grasp this concept.

In today's modern industrial real estate arena, the onus is on the tenant to take care of the property as if they own it, whether that maintenance is done with internal facility management staff or with external vendors. Sometimes, the landlord will take care of the exterior property and bill the tenant; other times it is a mix. For instance, the tenant might take care of everything except for the roof. Most institutional landlords service the HVAC units themselves and bill the tenants for quarterly service. This is because the landlord may want to control any maintenance they think preserves the property's value.

In other instances, the landlord turns the HVAC units and roof over to you, expecting you to get them back into working condition at the end of the lease. Some tenants have a facility manager who already takes care of everything in the warehouse, so adding exterior building responsibilities to their duties is a minimal burden.

In industrial leases, electricity and janitorial services are always separately paid for by the tenant. The main reason for this is that each industrial tenant has their unique uses and needs, making it impractical for a landlord to predict and manage them on their own.

Eighty percent of the time, the type of lease you need is determined by the building you choose. For example, if a large institution owns your building, it is likely they already have a specific way of operating it. Multi-tenant industrial landlords usually take care of maintenance in business parks because it is essential to pool expenses to maintain the business park's image. In single-tenant buildings, there can be some flexibility.

The moral of the story is, you want to be very clear about what will become your responsibility during the lease negotiation.

OPERATING EXPENSES

Operating expenses are often referred to as "OpEx," "triple net expenses," or "net expenses." They are specific property tax, insurance, and common area maintenance expenses associated with the property. Sophisticated tenants and brokers ask for a breakdown of the operating expenses on an annual basis to ensure they are reasonable. When appropriate, ask for three years of historical operating expenses to see how they have trended over time. If you find that one of the operating expense sections is greater than it should be or has increased substantially over time, it warrants further investigation into how the landlord operates the property and what future pass-through expenses you can anticipate.

Prologis now incorporates all maintenance, repair, and replacement operating expenses within their new Clear Lease and places a cap on how much they can increase annually. This results in predictable monthly operating expenses. Due to Prologis's scale, they can forecast and control their expenses to the advantage of customers by taking a variable cost and transforming it into a fixed cost. This allows executives to refocus the time and attention of general managers and facility managers away from daily facility-related maintenance and toward business growth and operations.

EARLY OCCUPANCY

Early occupancy is the time you can use to move in to the property, set up furniture, and install IT cabling, equipment, and racking before you start paying rent. The key differentiator between early occupancy and free rent is that in early occupancy, you are granted nonexclusive possession of the space. This means the landlord retains partial possession, which is usually for the purpose of completing tenant improvements. As a result, landlords do not want tenants to be fully operational yet at this point.

Some landlords will want you to pay the operating expenses during this time, while others will not. We will cover this in more detail below, in the Rent Abatement section.

Early occupancy can also be a practical concession to start the lease on the first of the month, as opposed to starting the lease date mid-month.

Understanding the difference between early occupancy and rent abatement can help you identify what you want and when you should ask for it.

RENT ABATEMENT

This is more commonly called free rent. While the concept is simple, its application is nuanced. Free rent is a concession the landlord provides only if it is needed to attract the tenant to sign the lease. It is usually given at the start of the lease because that is when it can offset the tenant's substantial cash outlays and capital investments in construction, equipment, furniture, as well as double rent, if the tenant is paying for both buildings while they transition.

Landlords lose cash flow when they grant free rent, so they are sometimes more willing to give it when it is spread throughout the lease term. For instance, one month free each year.

Landlords routinely add a month of lease term to the total lease length for every free month given. We reference this approach by saying the landlord is giving free rent "inside the lease term" or "outside the lease term." For example, think of a five-year lease with two months of free rent. When free rent occurs inside the lease term, a sixty-month term results in two months free, and fifty-eight months paid after that. When free rent occurs outside the lease term, a sixty-month lease becomes a sixty-two-month lease, whereby the first two months are free and sixty months are paid after that.

As we discussed earlier, free rent is a concession landlords give to tenants to attract them to leasing the landlord's space. The market supply and demand dynamics will dictate when landlords offer free rent and in what quantities. You can rely on your broker to know which concessions are reasonable at your specific point in the market cycle.

In the sixteen years I have been helping clients negotiate industrial leases, I have found there is always room for some free rent. In the softest of markets, free rent can be plentiful, and back in the recession of 2008, we would regularly negotiate one to two months of free rent per year of lease. I remember our office negotiated a year of free rent on a six-year sublease during this time. That created an extra 6 percent boost to our bottom line in the first year.

There is usually one string attached to rent abatement to keep all parties' interests aligned: if you default on your obligations, you pay back the free rent in full, immediately. The reason for this is that you should not be able to negotiate concessions out of your landlord and then take the money and run. You have to fulfill your part of the bargain.

OPERATING EXPENSE ABATEMENT

If you can negotiate free rent, does that mean you will pay nothing to the landlord during that time? Or will you still need to pay the operating expenses? There have been countless misunderstandings and mismanaged expectations over this nuance. It is assumed by the real estate community that you will pay the operating expenses during any free-rent period unless explicitly stated otherwise, but often the uninitiated assume otherwise. If you include your request for operating expense abatement early within the negotiation, you have the best chance for success. This can be used as a bargaining chip, trading for another concession in many instances.

For example, if you pay $80,000 per month in rent for your 100,000-square-foot industrial building, and the operating expenses are $20,000 per month, do you not think it is essential to be crystal clear on whether or not you are obligated to pay this $20,000 per month bill for the three months of free rent your broker negotiated? Most tenants do not negotiate these often enough to know better, nor will junior brokers. Savvy senior brokers, on the other hand, will be all over this. Make sure to include language that states abatement of all base rent and operating expenses during any free-rent period. I make sure my clients are never surprised that the $60,000 credit they thought was coming to them was a misunderstanding.

TENANT IMPROVEMENTS

Tenant improvements (TIs) are modifications to the property that need to be done to make the property accommodate your business needs. This lease section defines who will design, perform, and pay for said modifications. Tenant improvements are costly and time-consuming, and as such, they can have such a disproportionate effect on the success of your negotiations. Therefore, we will devote an entire chapter to the topic, Chapter 9, so you can reference in depth as needed.

BUILDING CONDITION

Many leases will have a section called Condition, which states the building will be delivered to the tenant with all building operating systems in proper working order. In practice, I have found it is helpful to call out all specific building systems that are deficient. You do not want to tell the landlord their building is in terrible shape, because it shames them and does not provide them an opportunity to save face. You likely would not negotiate on it in the first place if it were in bad shape, so it is best to handle the issue delicately. Remember to do the following:

1. Mention the building's condition, honestly and early in the process, so the landlord knows they must fix these neglected maintenance items.
2. Make sure the landlord does not confuse the repair of deficient building systems with your tenant build-out needs.

Sometimes landlords mention their property renovation plans and then try to use their renovation cash contribution against you when negotiating tenant improvement allowances. For example, some smaller private landlords will say, "We are already spending $200,000 to renovate the property, and as a result, we should not have to give you as much tenant improvement allowance." It is helpful to differentiate deferred maintenance from tenant improvements, because the former is for the landlord's benefit and part of regular capital reinvestment. The latter is in the tenant's interest and specific to your use.

PARKING

Parking is a big deal in office leasing because you pay for each reserved and unreserved parking stall, and in parking structures, you pay for visitor validations. When leasing a warehouse, you do not need to deal with paid parking, as warehouses do not have parking structures. However, you still need to make sure you are clear on the amount of parking you can use when you are in a business park environment with other tenants.

Ask the landlord:

1. Are the parking spaces exclusive?
2. Can there be reserved parking?
3. Can work trucks be parked overnight?
4. Can tractor-trailers be stored in the yard?

5. Can the yard be fenced?
6. Is street parking allowed?

Some people see there is street parking available and then plan on using that for extra employee parking, but then later learn that the city will not count that toward their allotment. Or parking is not allowed, or their neighbor utilizes all of those spaces.

SECURITY DEPOSIT

We all know what a security deposit is. But how much security deposit is reasonable in the industrial market? The main factors to consider are:

1. The length of time the company has been in business
2. The company's income statement, balance sheet, and/or tax returns
3. The size of the landlord's tenant improvement contribution
4. The length of the lease

There are also different methods of payment and forgiveness of the security deposit when a more substantial one is required. When an extra security deposit is required, it is always helpful to inquire as to the specific reason for the landlord's demand so you can address it. On occasion, it is possible to pay the extra security deposit over time. Quite regularly, though, an additional security deposit can be given back to the tenant in the form of a rent credit on anniversary dates of the lease, provided you are in good standing throughout the duration of the lease.

No conversation on security deposits would be complete without mentioning the illusionary letter-of-credit concept, which is an idea that sounds good but is not practical. Tenants sometimes prefer to give their landlord a letter of credit from their bank. This letter states that the bank will restrict a specific portion of funds from the tenant's bank account, with express instruction that if the tenant defaults on their lease, the bank will wire those funds to the landlord. What could go wrong here? Well, plenty.

What if there is a dispute as to whether or not the tenant is actually in default? What if the tenant sues the bank for unnecessarily sending the funds to the landlord? Banks are risk-averse to these types of arrangements, and landlords are too. When it comes to security deposits, cash is king.

AGREE TO TERMS BEFORE YOU NEGOTIATE THE CONTRACT

Unfortunately, sometimes overly eager or aggressive people will try to move the lease proposal negotiation into the lease contract negotiation before all of the lease proposal terms have been agreed upon by both parties. When people try to move to the contract too quickly, it is usually because they think they can hammer out the rest of the details later in the contract. This approach is fraught with misunderstanding and a waste of time, as you should not be rehashing basic business terms during the legal term discussion.

Remember, the purpose of the lease proposal is to size up your landlord's ability to accommodate your needs, without forcing them to negotiate unnecessarily. The contents of your lease proposal should focus purely on that purpose. It is also practical to make sure everyone is in full agreement with deal terms before both parties start incurring costly legal fees in contract negotiation.

DEAL ANALYSIS

Everyone has their own opinion as to what a good deal means to them. They go about using that lens to select properties and negotiate accordingly. The first and most obvious criterion for what constitutes a good deal is that it fulfills all of your minimum requirements operationally, financially, and from a timing perspective. You should compare multiple viable opportunities to inform your decision-making and to refine your analysis. The focus of your deal analysis can then show the impact of any proposed piece of real estate on your ability to operate profitably and grow the business.

Most people do not analyze their proposals or compare them in great detail. Some people will only compare the very last proposal in a negotiation. The first mindset shift I have found to be helpful is to track economics starting with the first proposal. Negotiating lease proposals can take a few—up to a dozen—rounds of negotiation, depending on the extent of the construction necessary. When you begin the process knowing the value of each prospective lease as it relates to another, you can make more refined value judgments.

Deal analysis is pretty straightforward on the landlord side of the table, as landlords make a capital investment in the acquisition of the property and then look for a return on that investment. Ultimately, there is a time when they sell the property, maximize its value, and maximize the overall yield of their investment. As I learned from one of my favorite UCLA professors, Karen Davidson, in the Argus discounted cash flow analysis class, when you can model each lease, you can understand how it affects the value of the property. This is helpful, as landlords are hyperfocused on this point.

HOW TO COMPARE MULTIPLE ALTERNATIVE LOCATIONS

The most common predicament executives find themselves in when their business needs to move to a new building is figuring out the best place to move it. As such, we will focus on how companies should compare multiple locations.

First, we start by comparing all of the proposals side by side. This analysis allows us to have internal discussions with our clients and to make value judgments based on real-time data. These value judgments then enable us to prioritize our pursuits and understand how we can leverage our next round of negotiations.

Some companies do very little lease analysis. Others have a series of complicated internal calculations based upon Financial Accounting Standards Board (FASB) guidelines, costs of capital, internal rates of return, and disclosure requirements. These calculations make you aware of how you can use fundamental financial analysis to improve decision-making.

Key inputs for proposal analysis on an industrial lease transaction are:

- Square footage
- Start date
- Term
- Starting rent
- Annual escalations
- Free rent
- Type of lease
- Base year
- Operating expenses

- Tenant improvement cost
- Tenant improvement allowance
- Net tenant improvement expense
- Tenant improvement amortization

The outputs then become:

- Year one annual cash flow
- Year one monthly cash flow
- Total value of concessions
- Net effective rent per square foot (this is the average rent per square foot after subtracting leasing concessions)
- Average cash flow per year
- Total consideration

If all you do is compare and contrast each of these inputs and outputs side by side within a spreadsheet, you will still be ahead of most people who operate based on gut feel.

DATA-DRIVEN DECISION-MAKING

To delve deeper into analysis and draw further insights, take the inputs and outputs and relate them back to your company's internal key performance metrics.

Here are some factors to take into account as you analyze your lease deal.

PROFIT AND LOSS IMPACT

It is helpful to compare how your profit and loss (P&L) statement will be impacted by each building. Perhaps you can hold more inventory in one of the warehouses, ship faster with a greater amount of loading docks in the second, and package goods faster in the third. It is helpful to create categories for each part of your business if you think they will be impacted significantly by one building over another. In doing this, you can then make value judgments and incorporate those value judgments into your negotiation. This shifts the tone of the conversation with the landlord from "market" deal negotiation to negotiation based on the property's value to *you*.

TIME

Time can be factored in many different ways: term lengths, construction timelines, lease commencement dates, and expiration dates, for starters.

- Term length: Double-check to see if all of the lease terms you are considering are the same length of time. Sometimes, concessions will lead to adding term onto the leases. You will want to assess if the added term works better or worse for you.
- Construction time: Project when each building will be deliverable based on the completion of tenant improvements. Check how confident you are in each landlord's ability to perform on time.
- Lease commencement time: Figure out the ideal month to start your lease. You might find two buildings that fit your company, but one landlord will push your start date out by only thirty days due to competing offers, whereas the other landlord can wait ninety days because of an existing tenant. Determine how flexible each landlord is to accommodate your timing.
- Expiration date: You may not want to end your lease during your busy season. Verify that the landlord can accommodate your desired lease expiration date.

TOTAL COST TO OCCUPY

For a review of the total cost to occupy the property, go back to Chapter 4 and review the three components of budgeting. For each lease, make sure you document:

1. The cost to build out the new building
2. The cost of the actual relocation
3. The cost to surrender and decommission the old building

You can then total these and understand the total cost to occupy each building in relation to the others, and determine how that affects a property's attractiveness to you.

EVALUATE YOUR LEASE RENEWAL

The cost to find a new building and relocate to it is almost always higher than the cost of extending your current lease. Moving within the same geographic area purely to get a better rent structure for the same size building almost never happens. If we are talking about moving out of state, then there is another set of considerations.

It is valuable to compare lease renewal versus relocating, because it is an opportunity to reframe your conversation with your landlord. When you tell your landlord you cannot renew with them because the value of the property to you is only X and they are asking Y, and you have studied the opportunity to relocate to a different building, you change the nature of the negotiation. Most people ask themselves, "Am I getting a good deal compared to all the other deals in the market?" With our approach, you shift the question to "What is this particular deal worth to *me*?" When the landlord understands this, it usually prompts them to become more creative in their deal making so they can better accommodate your unique needs.

The main difference between renewing your existing lease and relocating to a new building, other than forgoing the time and expense of finding, negotiating, building out, and relocating to the new building, is the cost and disruption of renovating your existing space if you choose to stay.

When companies make lease renewal decisions in five- to ten-year increments, they realize they will likely need to improve their space with every lease as well. This can be as minor as new paint and carpet, but usually there is a reorienting of office space to modernize the layout, accommodate new furniture, or make the space more efficient.

When considering renovations to your existing space, there are a few key considerations:

- The length of construction
- The impact on the use of space during construction
- Maintaining business continuity during construction
- The landlord's contribution to the renovation budget
- Whether or not the landlord's contribution will cover the entire budget
- Who will hire the contractor and manage the project
- The need for new furniture and associated costs
- Where existing team members will relocate during construction

Renovations can work in different ways. Some tenants have the landlord's construction crew renovate at night, so they do not disrupt the business during the day. Other companies move employees upstairs when their warehouse has a two-story office space, while the downstairs office is renovated. Sometimes, the landlord owns other property nearby where employees can be relocated temporarily. None of these options are fun, but they are worth it if they help you stay in your current property, save on the up-front costs of moving, and set your company up for growth for another five to ten years.

In the previous chapter, we talked about looking for deferred maintenance on potential new buildings to make sure landlords account for them apart from your tenant improvement budget. This will apply to your lease renewal negotiation as well.

LEASING VERSUS BUYING

Most companies know when they want to lease or own their building. If you are in doubt about which option you should pursue, chances are you still have detailed internal discussions to complete before entering into the market.

When it comes to large public and private companies, the decision to lease or buy usually revolves around how important the facility is to the company's mission. Corporate headquarters, for instance, are usually owned because they are viewed as mission critical to the company's success.

The same mission-critical idea applies to capital-intensive businesses. If you run a food production company, an automotive manufacturing plant, or any other operation where the up-front capital investment is unlikely to be paid back during the initial term of the lease, then you will likely want to own your property. The last thing you want is for your lease to expire and then your landlord deciding not to renew it or charging you excessive rent to remain in the property.

For private companies, there are a whole host of tax incentives designed to benefit property owners that you can take advantage of. These incentives range from writing off mortgage interest and property taxes to taking depreciation deductions and minimizing capital gains taxes. Oftentimes, the executive's CPA is the one who will change the opinion of the executive from leasing to buying after discussing specific tax advantages.

LEASE ACCOUNTING STANDARDS

No discussion of leases would be complete without touching on the fluid lease accounting standards implementation. Over the past decade, the FASB has been working with industry players to establish a new standard for lease accounting. The chief goal is to provide clarity on lease obligations within a corporation's financial statements. The highest-profile example of wrongdoing in this area is the Enron scandal of 2001, where Enron fooled investors through fake holdings and accounting practices that were off the books. An MBA student typically studies the Enron implosion in their second year, whereby they follow the history of the company's wrongdoings through their SEC reporting footnotes, which read like a fiction novel.

The problem FASB is looking to solve is that operating leases currently do not have to be disclosed on a company's financial statements. Real estate leases under fifteen years of length are classified as operating leases, whereas longer leases are considered capital leases. The difference between the two has to do with how the lease obligation is reported on the company's financial statements. This may not be a big deal for smaller, privately held companies. However, for any company that is public or relies on external capital sources, it is imperative for investors to understand all of a company's financial obligations. This allows them to assess risk and compare against other companies with transparency.

By implementing lease management software, companies can turn an opaque and tangential financial statement reference into data that is extracted, standardized, and available to investors.

PRIORITIZATION AND VALUE JUDGMENTS

Once you have made your matrix showing the qualitative and quantitative aspects of each building side by side, you can have an educated conversation to fine-tune your negotiation action plan. You are able to discuss how each variable changes a building's value to your company and prioritize those variables. It is through prioritization that one drives value.

Conversations usually take the tact of:

- If we choose this building, then we need to be concerned with X.
- If we choose the other building, then it is only worth Y to us.
- If we choose the third building, we effectively limit our growth to Z number of employees.
- Based on feedback from the broker and an updated analysis, I think we should go back to landlords A, B, and C with the following terms, X, Y, and Z.

The cycle of lease proposal negotiations, analysis, and internal meetings will require iterations as many times as necessary. I have seen some clients make the decision in one meeting; others

I have seen repeat the cycle six or seven times. Eventually, you will arrive at a point where each proposal reaches its limit, and it is time to make a final decision. Then you call the other party and utter those words that signal commitment:

"Let us go to lease documents."

"Please proceed."

"We are in agreement."

"Let us ink it."

"I will call my attorney and give him the go-ahead to draft the lease."

"I will have my attorney call your attorney."

You are now one step closer to the realization of your goal. The probability of success increases exponentially at this point, and all you need to do is make sure the lease has everything written correctly. Sound simple? Not so fast. Right when everything looks hopeful, it is time to prepare yourself for lease negotiations.

CHAPTER 8

TAILOR-MADE LEASES

Congratulations! You have a lease proposal that pleases both sides, and you are ready to begin lease negotiations. In this chapter, I will lay out the strategies and tactics I have used most frequently in my experience of negotiating more than five hundred commercial real estate transactions. This practical experience can provide you with some context as to how you will handle your lease negotiation. It can also help your in-house counsel prioritize critical sections of the lease.

One disclaimer: I am not an attorney. The information contained in this book is not legal advice and is provided for informational purposes only. You should hire a real estate attorney to advise you on how the law relates to your specific and unique situation.

NEGOTIATION STRATEGY
NEGOTIATING BASELINE

First, you should understand who is on your team and what they do. Let us start with the players on each side of the table. Depending on your company size, you may do everything, or you may have an outside attorney, an in-house counsel, or a whole real estate department. What is most important here is that you have a comfort level with the document, the type of transaction being contemplated, and an understanding of its effects on your business. Clear delineation of rights and responsibilities during the negotiation process can save you from years of problems later.

The size of the landlord's team is entirely dependent on the size and scope of the landlord's resources. Many landlords may have a broker prepare all of the lease documents using industry-standard, fill-in-the-blank contracts, most of which originate from the American Industrial Real Estate Association (AIR CRE). These AIR CRE contracts are the most balanced commercial lease contracts on the market. Everyone in the industry knows the AIR CRE lease document inside and out. I would feel comfortable signing the AIR CRE lease document as either a landlord or a tenant, knowing it could be easily modified to encompass the spirit of the negotiation between the two sides.

Most institutional and larger private landlords often have their lease contracts custom-crafted by a prominent law firm. It is common knowledge throughout the legal profession that the person writing the contract starts with a better negotiating position. The drafting party sets the first set of expectations for each right and responsibility.

INITIAL LEASE REVIEW

Once you have received the lease document from your landlord, it is time for your internal review. Start by making sure all of the business points have made it into the contract. As you read each section, make a note each time you have a question or concern. For perspective, think through how these notes are related and how to address them. Lastly, think about how each question or concern affects the other party and why it is there in the first place.

When you purchase a property, it is vital to have a clean transfer of ownership. When you lease property, you want a clean transfer of possession and a clear set of instructions for each party's rights, responsibilities, and obligations over time. Within a five- to ten-year lease, a lot of things can happen, and attorneys make a living contemplating what to do in each scenario.

For example, during a ten-year lease, the following can happen:

- The building systems go out of service.
- The ownership changes, and the new owner makes significant capital expenditures.
- Hundreds of different people may visit the property, and one of them may suffer an injury.
- Manufacturing processes may use multiple different chemicals, resulting in concerns about hazardous material migrating onto the property.
- The company leasing the building could be purchased and taken over by another company.
- Hail, hurricanes, and heat waves could affect the roof and landscaping.
- Trucks and trailer stands could damage the concrete and asphalt.

The lease document is an attempt to cover all contractual obligations for each party so there is no ambiguity. But, in reality, there is always ambiguity. Once again, there are volumes of lease negotiation books and guides that break down the aspects of each sentence of each clause of each type of lease. The purpose here is to make sure you have a baseline understanding of the most commonly negotiated sections, so you can ask the right questions of your team members.

NEGOTIATING POINTS AND TACTICS
PARTIES

Getting the right entities on the lease seems obvious. The concept of "who" is on the contract can get more complicated, because a company may change its name, legal entities, and stock ownership as it grows.

On the most basic level, we have the sole proprietor, who may not have a legal entity at all. If this is you, you might be surprised to know that some states and landlords require your spouse to sign the lease, even if he or she is not a part owner of the business. If this happens to you, protect yourself and your family by forming a legal entity to be on the lease. You might still have to personally guarantee the contract the first time; however, a thoughtfully negotiated agreement can sunset your personal guarantee over time, provided you remain current on your lease obligations up until then.

The next type of growth we commonly see is a fledgling startup with a legal entity that changes ownership structure as it raises capital. It may not matter to you that you are raising money for your company, but it may matter to the landlord, who wants to make sure you are financially viable to fulfill the lease contract. Most leases include standard language that says that if the majority ownership stake changes, the landlord can request financials from the new majority owner to ensure they are as stable as the original owner. Sometimes it is possible to strike this language from the lease, but it usually has to be explained in a way that reassures the landlord.

The middle market broadly consists of mature companies that have a corporate legal entity in one state and a separate legal entity in every other state where they conduct business. Which legal entity should be on the lease? Does the local entity stand on its own? Does the corporate body have to guarantee the contract? There is no one answer here. Some local entities report to corporate, and their financial statements consolidate into the parent company's financials. Other firms have each legal entity stand alone as a separate profit center. It is essential to communicate to your landlord how your company is structured.

We sometimes work with Fortune 500 companies that might go public or private throughout their tenure at a property. Public companies are heavily regulated and provide quarterly and annual SEC reports, subject to generally accepted accounting principles (GAAPs) to ensure transparency in their financial statements. That said, public companies can still have subsidiaries and elaborate corporate structures that are not nearly as transparent.

Sometimes it can be hard to demonstrate the financial viability of a subsidiary when their entity-level financials are not available. Private-equity-owned firms are a great example. This opaqueness is usually to your benefit as a tenant, in that you can ride the coattails of your corporate parent's financials. However, what if the corporate entity spins off your business unit? Could it default by being of lesser credit? You will want to think about your relationship with the corporate legal entity and its long-term viability.

Expect the landlord's attorney to double-check that your entity exists, ask what state it is registered in, and require proof of good standing by your respective secretary of state. Proof of good standing for corporations and limited liability corporations can be found quickly on the state's business search portal. However, confirming good standing for limited partnerships can take weeks, since they have to be manually verified by the secretary of state.

Providing proof of good standing seems simple enough, but things can get hung up on occasion.

In one instance, I helped a client renew their 40,000-square-foot warehouse lease in Charlotte, North Carolina. We spent months negotiating a lease extension, going through contract negotiations, tenant improvement negotiations, and the signing of the lease. The landlord's attorney checked if our entity was in good standing at the last moment and found out it was not.

However, we had been doing business in the state of North Carolina for ten-plus years, and as luck would have it, the state did not have some of our paperwork on file from seven years ago. The state had audited their records and changed our status from current to suspended without notice. After some due diligence, we rectified this hiccup, the landlord promptly signed the lease, and everybody was happy. The moral of the story is that the smallest of details can sometimes hold things up. By starting early and being organized, you can overcome such roadblocks with little to no pain. In this instance, if we had been relocating instead of renewing, this delay may have had cascading consequences.

SQUARE FOOTAGE

Roughly 5 percent of the time, tenants question the measurement of the warehouse being evaluated. As I shared earlier, if you ask five different architects to measure the same building, you will end up with five different building sizes. The difficulty of having 100 percent confidence in the exact square footage leads to a practical reality: you need to do your own due diligence to make sure the building is approximately the marketed size. If you want to watch a deal die quickly, dispute the square footage with a tape measure. Usually, the best remedy when there is a square footage concern is to run it by your architect. If you do not have one, ask you broker if one of his favorite architects will look at it as a favor.

One of my favorite UCLA instructors, Bryan Mashian, Esq, taught me you need to know that the square footage is the right order of magnitude, rather than the exact square footage, so you can focus on total dollars of the total square feet.

BOMA sums up this challenge in the opening statement of their guide on building measurements: "Due to the sheer variety of architectural designs, space configurations, and business requirements found in today's Industrial and Flex Buildings, this (BOMA) standard goes into great detail in order to cover as many real-world building conditions as possible. It is not possible to cover every conceivable permutation."

LANDLORD WARRANTY

The Condition section will customarily state that the landlord shall deliver all building systems of the property in working order. You obviously need to ensure the building is in good condition. However, it is not always practical to inspect every facet when vetting properties, so leases address this in the Condition section.

In most leases, there is a thirty-day grace period for the tenant, called the landlord's warranty. This warranty period states the landlord will be responsible for fixing any part of the building systems that are not in proper working order, if notified by the tenant during the warranty period. When it comes to the HVAC system, this warranty period may be as short as thirty days, or upward of six months. Some landlords will try to forgo this warranty altogether. I have negotiated lease warranty periods from one year up to five years in some cases. This warranty is an item that is not usually settled in the lease proposal but rather negotiated by experienced brokers in particular circumstances.

HAZARDOUS MATERIALS

You want to make sure you are only responsible for the hazardous materials you bring onto the property and that you handle and dispose of them in a professional manner that does not damage the property.

Experienced industrial tenants, brokers, and investors have dealt with industrial properties that have an environmental history. Selling a property that has active or former environmental contamination can be extremely challenging. Leasing a property that has or has had environmental contamination can be possible under the right circumstances.

My favorite environmental consultant is Steve Figgins of EKI Environment & Water. I have known him for over a decade and rely on his expertise regularly. In an interview, Steve explained that vapor intrusion is the most common environmental issue facing companies in industrial buildings today. Subsurface vapor occurs when a solvent spills onto a concrete slab and seeps through the concrete, turning into vapor underneath the slab in the soil. In extreme circumstances, it flows down into the groundwater.

With subsurface vapor concerns, a landlord will have to test the soil through borings and conduct indoor air monitoring tests. If the test results come back below a specific level as mandated by your city, county, or state guidelines, then it may not be of concern for your daily operations. However, if the levels are near or above the threshold, then the landlord may have to install a depressurization system and an additional air handling system to ensure a safe environment for daily human work.

Vapor intrusion can also happen as a result of underground storage tank leaks, but these most often occur in the yard area of an industrial property, with less potential for harmful consequences to human life.

I have found that some tenants arrive at a comfort level if the property is safe, whereas others will wholesale abandon any leasing efforts on a property if there is even a whiff of environmental concerns whatsoever. It is important to ask the question first. Second, verify the property's environmental background by searching the address on your state water resource control board database. The one for California is called GeoTracker. Here you will find known environmental issues and read through the property's historical cleanup actions, regulatory activities, environmental data, site maps, and community involvement records.

When in doubt, and in instances of larger and longer lease transactions, it might be advisable to conduct a Phase I study, and potentially a Phase II environmental assessment, prior to entering into a lease. The purpose of conducting such assessments is to have a clear delineation of the condition of the property before and after you take possession, so there is a clear chain of title for any site conditions.

You do not want to be subject to unhealthy conditions, and you do not want to be held liable for your landlord's past environmental contamination. If you sense this is something of concern, you will want to engage an environmental consultant and an environmental attorney to review the property you are interested in leasing.

TENANT IMPROVEMENTS

We will talk more about tenant improvements in the next chapter, but here is a brief overview in the context of negotiations. There are three underlying conditions in which you will find office space within industrial buildings: as is, shell condition, and fully renovated.

When a tenant moves out of an industrial building, the landlord has to decide whether to renovate the office before finding a new tenant. The smaller the landlord or property, the higher the likelihood they will conserve cash and wait for a new tenant to tell them what they want. This means there could be holes in the walls, dirty carpet, worn linoleum, non-ADA-compliant bathrooms, and damaged ceiling tiles. In this instance, most landlords expect to paint and carpet the space, refurbish any parts of the office that need new surfaces, and replace damaged ceiling tiles. We call the condition of such a space at turnover to the new tenant "as is."

Shell-condition space exists when an investor purchases an industrial building, repositions it, and puts it back out to market for lease-up. If the building has a significant office space component, the investor will demo the existing office, replace the ceiling and lighting components, repair and paint all interior walls, and leave the floor as raw concrete. When you walk into the building, all you will see is one clean, white, wide-open space. This is called a "vanilla shell" or "shell" condition. An investor will then budget for an office build-out for the new tenant.

Fully renovated office space usually exists with institutional landlords with warehouses of less than 10,000 square feet of office. The reason this is suited for institutional landlords is that they see their spaces as a direct reflection of their company, and they want their spaces to lease for the highest rate possible. The landlord takes the creative design component out of the leasing process by having the space renovated and ready to lease. Landlords find that a fully renovated space makes it easy for prospective tenants to see the space and say, "Yes, that works; we will take it."

A note on office renovations: landlords used to wait to put flooring in until the tenant picked out their type and color of carpet. This process used to be widespread, as some sole proprietors have specific tastes or company colors. Today, interior design has become so sophisticated, it has become more of an asset for the landlord to hire an architect to spec out all or part of the office. Standard finishes for modern buildings are becoming higher end than executives would choose on their own, and landlords are using this for a competitive advantage. For example, many are installing luxury vinyl tile throughout common areas or polishing the concrete instead of keeping the standard flooring.

If you are going to modify the current office space to fit your company, it is essential for you to be very specific about what you want, who is going to pay for it, who is going to build it, and when. As construction is one of the most natural places where landlords and tenants have misaligned expectations, we will delve more deeply into tenant improvements in the next chapter.

REPLACEMENT OBLIGATIONS

The responsibility of replacing building systems as needed varies by the lease contract. Some tenants maintain that it is the landlord's building; therefore, the landlord should be responsible for replacing all building systems, just like apartment landlords. However, landlords maintain that because the tenant is using each building system while they occupy the property, it should be the tenant's responsibility. The most likely outcome is the tenant being responsible for replacing any building systems they have direct control of.

The most common use of this replacement clause is with the replacement of HVAC units. What if one of the units dies after you have been in the building for two years? Do you call your landlord to notify them, and they replace it? Or do you have to replace it at your own cost, with your own vendor? The answer is different in each lease. An HVAC unit costs $5,000 to $20,000, depending on the unit's locale, type, and tonnage. It is one thing for one HVAC unit to break, but what if you are like my client with a laboratory that has twenty HVAC units? If each HVAC unit lasts fifteen years, he might be replacing four HVAC units some years.

Before you replace an HVAC unit, first make sure you know when a replacement is required. The standard language and expectation for HVAC replacement is when the cost of repair is greater than 50 percent of the cost of replacement. I have found this logic to be acceptable to both sides.

Next, who fronts the cost for the replacement? The standard AIR lease language stipulates the landlord contracts and pays for the HVAC replacement. The landlord is then able to bill the tenant for a portion of the cost. The expense the tenant is responsible for is proportionate to the length of the lease divided by the HVAC's useful life, which is generally considered to be twelve years.

As with everything else in the lease process, there is nuance here too. Some lease language states that the numerator is the total length of the lease term. Other leases say the numerator is the total amount of time left on the lease at the time of replacement. Let us use an extreme example to make it easy to understand the ramifications of the two approaches.

Let us say you have a six-year lease. Halfway through it, you have two HVAC units that need to be replaced, for a total of $10,000. If you have the term of the lease as the numerator, you are responsible for reimbursing your landlord for six-twelfths, or 50 percent, which would total $5,000. If you have remaining lease term language in your lease, then you would be responsible for three-twelfths worth of the replacement, which would be 25 percent, or $2,500. If you have twenty HVAC units and have to replace every one, the difference is $50,000.

When negotiating the lease, you must frame this issue in the context of proportionality. You might be okay with being responsible for paying for a portion of the new HVAC unit's useful life but not paying for part of the new unit while you still have the old unit. While accounting standards define twelve years as the useful life of an HVAC unit, many companies will tell you they can last up to twenty-five years if properly maintained. Why should you be responsible for paying for the old unit once it is past its useful life? If you do that, the landlord might have had a prior tenant pay for the HVAC unit already, and you are paying them again for that same unit. The replacement of building systems should be structured as an equitable sharing of expenses, not a way for someone to make a profit.

SUBLEASING

As we discussed earlier, you need to be familiar with subleasing, as this will be your primary method of ending your occupancy if you find you no longer require the property mid-lease.

A distribution client in Memphis, Tennessee, had a West Coast distribution in Cerritos, California. We had been working together for ten years and had a handful of leases under our belt when the CEO called me. He said a conglomerate had purchased his largest customer, and the acquirer intended to take distribution in-house. That meant that in three months, my client would have zero need for the Cerritos warehouse and would be stuck paying $12,000 a month for the next forty-eight months.

We immediately put the building on the market for sublease. Being in the market every day, we knew there was excessive demand for space, and people would come to us from all over the county, as the building was centrally located. Downtown Los Angeles was twenty miles north, the two largest ports in the United States were twenty miles west, Orange County was twenty miles south, and the Inland Empire distribution hub was just twenty miles east. We were able to leverage that activity and got our neighbor to provide an offer to lease our space for seven years at a higher rent than our current contract.

We took this proposal and the financials to the landlord. Now we had the landlord's attention. Upon the lease signing with the new tenant, we signed a termination with the landlord, effectively canceling our lease. My client was happy to mitigate the budget impact of his customer's loss by getting out of the satellite Cerritos warehouse lease. We were also able to negotiate with the neighbor to buy the forklift and furniture to relieve our client from the trouble of shipping them back to corporate headquarters.

The alternative to terminating the lease would have been a traditional sublease. In a sublease, we would have remained liable for the next forty-eight months, hoping the subtenant paid the rent. We knew we would be responsible for rent if the subtenant went under. We would also have to work with the subtenant on future repairs, deal with issues between the two parties as they arose, collect and hold on to a security deposit, and so on, while the landlord would continue to hold on to our security deposit. At the end of the lease, we would deal with surrender of the property, walk-throughs, restoration, and so on. Instead of spending all of this time with the subtenant, the executive could focus on rebuilding the company.

When you are negotiating the lease document, you cannot count on the future prospect of terminating the lease. You also need to protect yourself in the event that you actually need to sublease the space. Remember, even if you have subleased your space, you are still responsible for it until you and your new subtenant have fully discharged all of the obligations of the lease.

The first key terms to negotiate in the Sublease section are the amount of time and the cost of the landlord's approval of your new subtenant. Some leases will give the landlord too much time to review the sublease request, where others will allow for their sole discretion to approve of subtenants. Usually, you can arrive at a fair amount of time, and your requirement to wait for their approval is released if they go over their allotted time.

You will also find that the landlord will want the ability to charge you for their own time, effort, and attorney to review any sublease request. Many leases do not cap these expenses. It is helpful to arrive at a fair flat-fee amount or an amount "not to exceed." These expenses are per occurrence, so if you try to sublease your space once and it does not work out, you will pay this fee again with each attempt. This is fair, as it does take time and effort to review each request.

AMERICANS WITH DISABILITIES ACT

Everyone agrees the Americans with Disabilities Act (ADA) is essential, as it ensures that buildings provide a clear path of travel for people with disabilities and that they will be able to access the property. Accessibility is not limited to the entrance to the building. It encompasses the parking lot, sidewalk, all doors, the downstairs and upstairs office, restroom stalls and sink areas, and the entire building. The ADA code is occasionally updated, so accessibility must be upgraded on a periodic basis.

The tension with ADA upgrades usually revolves around who is responsible for making those upgrades, and when. Most tenants think the landlord should be responsible because it is their building. The landlord's view is that a building must be compliant when it is built, and every tenant who inhabits the building should be responsible for making upgrades required for their own specific use.

A good way to estimate who will bear the cost of an ADA upgrade is to find out if the building will require construction, regardless of who is going to occupy it next. Then, it is usually practical for the landlord to make these improvements. Construction requires permits, and permits require ADA inspection, so this is the trigger point for this discussion in negotiations. If, on the other hand, the building does not require any ADA upgrades for a new tenant, but the tenant's use has a special component (such as being open to the general public) then the tenant will likely be responsible for these improvements.

GUARANTORS

The general premise is that if the entity that you want on the lease document is new, or if the size of the obligation you are taking on is large, the landlord will look for an additional guarantor. The guarantor is a separate entity that agrees to take on the obligation of the lease if the original lease signatory defaults. The concept is the same as a co-borrower or cosigner on a loan.

Do mature companies need guarantors? They do in many cases. Business growth is not limited to the physical size of their building. Sometimes they grow by territory and geographic markets. As a business starts operating in multiple cities, states, and countries, they start spending more time and resources structuring their legal entities. We find that mature companies may need to guarantee leases for newly opened locations, for exceptionally large warehouses, and when asking for significant tenant improvement allowances from landlords.

Most lease forms state that if the parent company sells the subsidiary, the parent company is no longer obligated to guarantee the lease. Conceptually, this makes sense, as a parent company should not have to continue to secure the lease of a company it no longer owns. On the other hand, landlords need more protection than just the local branch, so they often leave this release language out of their own custom-drawn legal documents. But can the landlord try to dictate that the parent company has to assign the guarantee to the new parent company? I have found we can usually negotiate so the parent company never has to guarantee the lease in the first place, and the lease remains guaranteed by the company set to occupy the property.

Guarantees are a given; the question is what you can and should exclude from them. We always make sure officers of the company are not guaranteeing the lease personally, and sometimes we will negotiate the tenant improvement expenses out of a guarantee. Lastly, we will ask to have the guarantee expire before the lease expires, or have the guarantee expire after the original term expires but prior to any extensions.

LEASE OPTION TO EXTEND

You do not have to be in the business long to hear someone say they want a two-year lease, and three one-year options to extend the lease. Tenants love asking for options. They feel like it is giving the landlord a concession—they are showing their intent to remain in the property, even if they are signing a short-term lease up front.

However, experienced brokers know that options are for the sole benefit of the tenant, not the landlord. An option obligates the landlord to keep you as a tenant if you would like to stay.

An option does not enable the landlord to keep you as a tenant if you wish to leave.

I consider lease options to be a low priority during most negotiations because they only serve as insurance for worst-case scenarios. I avoid asking for options because option language becomes so watered down, and the tenant does not really get anything other than a more restrictive set of rules that will dictate future lease negotiations.

Common lease option language states the following:

- In no event shall the new rental amount be lower than the prior rental amount.
- No tenant improvements shall be included.
- No free rent or leasing concessions shall be included.
- If you cannot agree to a rental amount with your landlord, you both must hire two appraisers, who then hire a third independent appraiser who will decide your fate through baseball arbitration.

Because of this restrictive language, I have found that 90 percent of the time my clients have an option, we choose not to use it, and we start a new negotiation from scratch. We can then go about assessing our needs through a fresh lens, understanding the landlord's motivations and striking a new deal that is good for everyone.

You still want to be prudent with how you time your new negotiations, though. It might be valuable to negotiate a new lease before your option to extend window opens. You should also know that some landlords may ask you to waive your option to extend in order to pursue new lease negotiations.

LOOKING FORWARD

We have walked through the main components of the lease document, which play a considerable role in enabling your company's success over the life of the lease. Now we can shift our focus to a more immediate concern: tenant improvements.

Tenant improvements have a dramatic and palpable influence on your company up front, on day one when everyone moves into the new building. Well-thought-out and well-executed tenant improvements dictate how employees feel when they come to work and impact how well they work together. We will consider how to maximize your tenant improvements in the next chapter.

CHAPTER 9

TENANT IMPROVEMENTS AND CONSTRUCTION

The joy of the industrial building is its versatility. And when it comes to warehouse leasing, there is no shortage of opportunities for creative problem-solving. We love helping clients figure out how to turn an old industrial building into a high-performance workplace. My team has helped repurpose property into new corporate headquarters, expand a laboratory to accommodate additional cancer research scientists, figure out how to better relocate household goods for military families through thoughtful design, and build out property so it can serve as corporate property today and investment property tomorrow. This creative problem-solving is one of the most fun ways we add value to our clients' experiences.

In this section, we will explore tenant improvements, which generally focus on office space. It is hard to separate the thought process of a tenant improvement negotiation during the lease proposal phase from the actual process of construction. You must be able to contemplate both at the same time to be successful. I recommend reading this section before the lease proposal phase, and then again after signing the lease but before construction begins. In the next chapter, we will give more consideration to optimizing your warehouse space.

Construction is relatively commonplace in industrial real estate. Renovations are prevalent because each company has unique needs. No two operations are the same. Trucking companies need driver rooms, manufacturers need to distribute electricity everywhere, and medical device companies need climate-controlled assembly areas. With every operation, we focus on what needs to be built for the company to grow. After focusing on a company's needs, we then focus on their wants. It is imperative to learn the difference when budgeting, so we can keep the right balance of form and function.

For smaller buildings and startups, adding an office here or there is all that is required. You do not have to have an architect to make modest space modifications. In these cases, you will find that the landlord will take care of this for you. Sometimes, you may want to do it yourself if the landlord will incentivize you with free rent or you have close friend who is a general contractor.

What follows is a broad overview of tenant improvements. If you would like to dig in more, my favorite book for executives is *Mistake Free Medical Office Design and Construction* by Richard Boureston. The author comes from a place of extreme knowledge but writes in a manner that is accessible to all skill levels. Even though this book focuses primarily on medical office space, 90 percent of the advice is relevant to all improvements.

My favorite textbook on this subject is *Construction Project Management: A Practical Guide to Field Construction Manage-*

ment by S. Keoki Sears, Glenn A. Sears, and Richard H. Clough. This book is a worthy read for team members working on multiple construction projects annually for larger companies.

SETTING EXPECTATIONS

Before we even tour a property with clients, we inquire with each landlord. It is immensely helpful to know who the landlord is and how they typically handle tenant improvements. We save countless hours per assignment when we vet landlords before spending client time touring properties.

Many private landlords, for instance, expect to provide little to no tenant improvements, and when they do, they take the form of "move a couple of walls." Many private landlords may still operate their portfolio in antiquated ways. These landlords own their property—they initially purchased it, and they ran their business from it. They kept their property after selling their business and retiring, and they now lease it out to new tenants. A private landlord often thinks that since they had to pay a contractor every time they built something within their warehouse, their tenants should too.

These landlords generally look at everything through the lens of minimizing outgoing cash flow. They will give free rent instead of making a cash contribution. Free rent is still a cash equivalent, but it simply delays incoming cash flow rather than increasing outgoing cash flow. These types of landlords can lead to difficult negotiations based more on personality than hard numbers. The upside, though, is these types of landlords can be more flexible and open to creative arrangements. This can lead to you being able to use your own contractor because he is a friend, paying half your security deposit now and half later, or even buying the building from the landlord halfway through your lease.

Institutional landlords, on the other hand, carefully consider operating budgets for tenant improvement allowances. This tenant improvement allowance is viewed as a cash equivalent, and in many cases, can be used in multiple different ways. These landlords will usually talk about tenant improvement allowances in terms of dollars per square foot. They know that building out office space from scratch can generally run fifty to seventy-five dollars per square foot for traditional office space and seventy-five to one hundred dollars per square foot for creative office space, and that paint and carpet typically run six dollars per square foot. Institutional investors manage other people's money, so they look at each dollar as an investment being put to work to earn a yield, which must be shielded from risk.

Private owners and institutional investors are but two types of landlords in the industrial market. Other kinds of ownerships include private equity funds, banks, developers, high-net-worth individuals, real estate investment trusts, grandmas and grandpas, grandchildren, estate attorneys, property syndicators, and dozens more. Each group has its own unique set of circumstances and common behaviors to consider when negotiating, especially as it pertains to tenant improvements. We focus on the private owner and institutional investor in this book, as they are most prevalent, but the lessons overlap most other ownership types.

The moral of the story is, do your homework on your potential landlord up front. Understand their expectations and how they compare to yours.

SPACE PLANNING

In my experience, 90 percent of people design a space that costs more than they can afford. It is in the refining of a space plan where value judgments are made and deals are negotiated. This is where an architect excels. The architect will help custom-fit your future space within your operational and financial requirements. Sometimes, the landlord will pay for the architect's services in hopes of creating a solution that will lead to a lease. Other times, you must foot the bill.

This part of the process will be iterative and can sometimes happen before you enter the market in the lease proposal phase, when the landlord delivers turnkey improvements, or after lease signing when you are simply negotiating a specific dollar amount. Architects will ask you detailed questions to understand your needs and then reflect upon them. These questions will center around your company culture and how your team uses its space to grow your company.

The architect will take your requirements and come up with a few prospective layouts for the spaces you are considering. In the best of scenarios, the different designs they provide are raw material for management discussions that can lead to creative solutions. This often results in a mixing and matching of ideas and layouts, combining the best of ideas.

You can usually revise the layout twice within a typical space-planning session. If the landlord is paying the architect, the landlord is doing so with the assumption that the space plan will create a solution that is the basis for a lease. If it seems like the tenant is not taking the process seriously or the scope spirals out of control, it can become the tenant's responsibility to pay for the rest of the architect's services.

Some landlords bypass this entire process and only deal with tenants who are willing to do their own space planning and improvements. In this case, the landlord will take the subject space and outfit it with standard building finishes, but that is the extent of their contribution. The landlord will provide a standard office layout that can be reused by most of the industry, and it is up to you to customize it for your operation. If this is the case, you might get a better economic deal, but you may also be responsible for removing whatever you build at the end of the lease.

Even after an architect has assessed your needs and designed an office space that works, the process is not over. Finishing a space plan can sometimes seem slow and arduous. You cannot finish a space plan without a bid. When you hear the term "value engineering," you are getting close. Value engineering means your architect and contractor will try to figure out ways to get you what you want with the budget you have.

It is hard for the landlord to issue firm lease terms before they know the cost of the construction project. Depending on whether it costs $50,000 or $250,000, their answer will be drastically different. Once you have designed and bid your TIs, then you can figure out who pays for what and the method of payment.

Think of your landlord as a bank. If they are going to spend their own money to build out your office space for you and they expect you to pay it back over time, they are essentially loaning you money. If the landlord is hiring and managing the contractor, they are also taking on risk and spending their own time as well. They will want to make sure they get an adequate return in exchange. Enter the architect's trusted tool: the pricing plan.

PRICING PLAN

Think of the pricing plan as the roadmap the architect is creating for the general contractor. The pricing plan will identify the parts of the existing office that are to be demolished, along with the planned office size, shape, finishes, materials, and quantities. The architect will then provide options for upgrades and alternatives for the contractor to bid as separate line items. Then the client and architect can go about mixing and matching to find the right balance of form and function. Again, this part of the process can happen during the lease proposal phase or during the construction phase, depending on who is paying for and performing the construction.

Some tenants think they can just call contractors, walk the space, and go straight to the bid without a space plan or a pricing plan. However, contractors will refuse to bid in this circumstance unless it is a tiny job or they are desperate for the work. Without a space plan and a pricing plan, the job is communicated differently to each contractor, and each bid will look dramatically different. Nobody wins when construction bids run this way.

Knowing the expected amount of tenant improvement allowance is just as important as knowing the condition of the space. The demolition part of the pricing plan helps bring more understanding here.

In many cases, the landlord is already planning on renovating the space to bring it up to code, modernize the base building systems, and/or remove old improvements. You should not have to use your tenant improvement allowance to fund this part of the project. Clarify with the landlord which funds are going toward demolition.

Remember, the established budget rental rate in the landlord's pro forma is what dictates the amount of funds the landlord will contribute toward your tenant improvements. They will respond to any request for increase in tenant improvement allowance with a commensurate increase in your rental rate. However, market conditions and negotiation strategies can cause exceptions to this rule.

We recently negotiated on a 21,000-square-foot warehouse with a public company in Santa Fe Springs, California. The building had 1,500 square feet of office, and the landlord was already planning on renovating the existing space. In this situation, we wanted to expand the office to 3,000 square feet. The landlord had an initial budget of $160,000 for tenant improvements. Could $160,000 build out the other 1,500 square feet of office that we needed? That $160,000 represented $107 per square foot. For that amount, the tenant figured they could build the nicest, newest office with exposed ceiling, new stainless-steel HVAC ducts, hanging circular LED lighting, Klein sliding glass doors, glass office walls, and polished concrete.

However, it turned out the $160,000 did not go that far because of the base building needs. Adding 1,500 square feet of office to the existing 1,500 square feet of office meant:

- New fire-rated walls were necessary to separate the offices from the warehouse.
- The original 1,500 square feet needed to be demolished to create the desired layout.
- The wheelchair ramp and bathrooms needed ADA upgrades.
- Building systems needed to be upgraded to ensure Title 24 compliance.

- The HVAC unit was too small to support the larger office and needed to be replaced.
- The sprinkler system required modification.

Through the space-planning process and further clarification in the pricing plan, we were able to design a layout to mitigate these challenges and come up with an agreement that worked for everybody.

CONTRACTOR BIDS

When you have a completed pricing plan, it is helpful to double-check that it is all-inclusive. Pricing plans usually involve interior improvements. You will also want to think about the exterior to make sure you have included any work that needs to be done within the project. It is easy to miss items that are out of sight and out of mind. Talk through the pricing plan to actively search for missing items, and then take your pricing plans to the general contractors and set up the job walk.

The job walk is the opportunity for general contractors to walk the space with the architect, tenant, landlord, project manager, or construction manager, and to inspect the area and compare it with the pricing plan. It is usually ideal to have three contractors bidding a job. If you only have two, you might not be able to triangulate realistic expenses or receive a credible bid. If you have more than three, you will create apathy amongst the bidders. All of the general contractors should be there simultaneously, which will create a mutual understanding of the job and give the general contractors an idea of who else is bidding. A general contractor bidding in a vacuum may result in higher pricing. A successful job walk results in accurate expectations.

Even with the most exacting pricing plan, there can still be ambiguity. When you inspect the three bids, you will notice they are often structured differently—so differently that sometimes we wonder whether the contractors were bidding the same job! Each general contractor has their own way of bidding.

There are a handful of things you should look for when examining bids, which are usually broken down by category of construction. Evaluate the assumptions and quantities the contractor includes within each category. Take that understanding and then look at each add-on. It is in comparing and contrasting bids that you will inevitably have questions. Most people question whether specific costs are allocated within a certain category. For example, are HVAC registers and returns included in the ceiling grid category or in the HVAC category?

With three bids, you can triangulate and ballpark expenses. What you look for are outliers. If one of the contractor's line items is twice as much as another's, it warrants investigation. It can be helpful to come up with a list of questions for each contractor to understand how they put their bid together and what they considered. You might find that your detailed pricing plan did not have everything needed for a comprehensive contractor bid after all. Sometimes you will have to ask each contractor to revise their pricing as a result.

TENANT IMPROVEMENT ALLOWANCE

Once the landlord has completed pricing your TIs, they can finalize how much they will contribute toward these improvements. This allowance will be based upon achieving a specific rental rate, including annual rental increases, and taking into account other requested leasing concessions. When it comes to spending the tenant improvement allowance, the allocation of funds can happen in a myriad of ways.

The first approach occurs when the landlord is in charge of the project: they use their own contractor and project management, and pay for the construction directly. The advantage of this is time savings, the landlord's expertise, and the potential pricing power if the landlord has several jobs with the same contractor. The disadvantage is that your money may not go as far, assuming the landlord charges management fees for overseeing the construction. If this is the case, then the contractor will have a fiduciary responsibility to serve their client, the landlord, instead of you, the tenant. A savvy landlord will budget the job and have the tenant pay for any expected overages up front. This up-front payment ensures the tenant has skin in the game.

The second approach allows you to be in charge of the construction, hire your own contractor, and pay for the construction directly. In this situation, we will negotiate a credit for free rent to help offset construction costs.

The third approach allows you to be in charge of the project with your own general contractor, but it is paid for by the landlord. This payment can take place in a lump sum with progress payments going directly to the contractor and the final payment occurring upon confirmation of contractor lien releases.

Small businesses that already have SBA loans may find that those loans can fund tenant improvements. SBA allowances may be structured such that the outstanding balance of the loan is interest-only during construction, and then converts to a principal-and-interest payment once the work is completed.

This is customary when small businesses purchase their own property and need to build it out.

Discuss with your broker which arrangement is best for you. Sometimes, we can structure a TI allowance that includes some IT infrastructure. Other times, we can use the TI allowance funds to install signage inside and outside of the property. And at other times, we can use it for audio and visual installations. Navigating this minutiae is where having an experienced internal team member, broker, or project manager will pay dividends and reduce surprises.

TENANT IMPROVEMENT AMORTIZATION

If the landlord is funding tenant improvements to build out your space, they will expect it to be paid back over time with interest. This premise is called amortization. The majority of the time, the payback period is the length of the lease—usually five years on buildings that are 10,000 square feet or larger. On longer leases, you might have a payback period that is shorter than the lease. Much like a loan, you have to balance the payback period with the interest rate and payment amount. You may want to pay it back as soon as possible to reduce the amount of interest you pay. Or you may want to minimize your payment and make it as low as possible on a monthly or annual basis. Some tenants pay back all of their TIs upon completion of construction.

Interest rates vary considerably throughout the industry. Some small landlords won't charge interest at all. They do whatever it takes to make a deal come together, while still getting their money back. The largest landlord in Southern California routinely charges 8 percent per year. Most experiences fall somewhere between the two extremes.

Many landlords use regular lending benchmarks when sizing up the interest rate, but if they do, make sure they are relevant benchmarks. A thirty-year fixed residential mortgage might be 3.75 percent, but a thirty-year mortgage is not directly comparable to a five-year commercial lease. Part of this process is to help you understand what is reasonable. You may find that your landlord already has a policy and thought process in place. If you want to deviate from that, you have to propose what you think is reasonable and be able to articulate your rationale for why your idea makes more sense.

WORK LETTER

Once you have designed your space, refined pricing through the pricing plan, negotiated the tenant improvement allowance amount and method of payment, it is time to document everything within the lease. This is where the work letter comes into play. The work letter dictates the tenant and landlord obligations relative to construction. Negotiating appropriate terms within the work letter will protect both tenant and landlord alike.

When it comes to the landlord performing construction, there is usually a targeted completion date. There could be a consequence if there is a delay, but it all has to do with what caused the delay and how controllable it was. The cause of delay might be weather, city regulations, disruption in the supply of materials and labor, change orders, and countless other influences. In general, if something outside the landlord's control causes the delay, the landlord is not penalized.

The most commonly agreed-upon remedy is to have the lease commencement date match the date when construction will be substantially complete. If the delay causes you to incur costs like having to hold over in your current space and pay double rent, or if it delays your relocation team, tensions will increase rapidly. We usually negotiate a drop-dead date within forty-five to sixty days from the estimated completion date. That way, if construction is incomplete, the tenant can terminate the lease. This is more of a last-resort tactic than a practical one because it is bad for both sides: tenants have already sunk considerable costs into the relocation endeavor, and landlords have spent money on construction with no tenant to pay it back.

We can always obtain a better result by improving project management and contingency planning, and increasing communication. Preparing for the risk of construction delay is another opportunity for an experienced team member, broker, or project manager to save you from considerable disruption.

PERMITS

The city will be an immovable force within the process at the beginning, middle, and end. The city usually gets thirty days from the receipt of a construction application to verify all of the appropriate documents were received. If there are missing documents or additional information is needed, they will notify you, wait to hear back, and then start the thirty-day period over again. Most city planners and building department officials are accessible in person at city hall. I recommend sending someone from your team to talk to city planners and building officials early in the process to ensure everything is in order.

The city inspector will be the head official visiting your job. Usually, they arrive before the interior walls are closed so they can inspect the electrical work. They will also do a final inspection, not only of your construction, but also of your racking and other equipment installations, before granting your certificate of occupancy.

City planners do valuable work, but they are not entrepreneurs. The nature of working for a municipality can mean that they are understaffed, closed for lunch, and closed every other Friday. They may answer their incoming calls, or they may sometimes reply to voicemails on another day, as they usually have a long line of people at their counter. This means your team will have to cater to the planning department to make sure everything goes smoothly. This will be your general contractor, project manager, or superintendent, depending on the issue. Going to the city in person is always helpful but time-intensive. Leverage your team here. Over time, your team will get a feel for what to expect from the inspector and can take these factors into consideration during future construction projects.

I have found that the right architect will have relationships with people in the zoning, planning, and building departments and can expedite your efforts more than any other person. It is helpful to communicate with your architect early and often to understand the city's current workflow and backlog. This will give you a more accurate estimate for your construction timeline.

STORAGE DURING CONSTRUCTION

While the contractor is constructing the office space, sometimes it will help your cause substantially if you can use a portion of the warehouse to receive new furniture, store excess inventory, and start your transition. Entrepreneurial landlords may be amenable to this arrangement, but most institutional landlords have too many concerns about safety and security to agree to this.

Landlords do not want to be responsible for your company's personal property while they are in possession of the building. It would require a whole new agreement just to draft all the "what if" risk scenarios. A good moving and storage vendor can help you avoid this issue.

If you are going to store materials in the building, make sure they are secure, lower-value items. Sometimes you can use a portion of the warehouse that is not accessible to the area under construction. Sometimes you can just use the outdoor fenced yard and drop containers. Other times, you can put an inexpensive chain-link fence around your warehouse property. Where there is a will, there is a way.

CONTRACTOR PAYMENT AND COST OVERRUNS

Construction projects frequently have unexpected costs, so you will want to think through how to deal with them in advance. Cost overruns are not usually because of a greedy and aggressive contractor who loves change orders. They usually occur because of changes made during construction and unforeseen conditions. Once clients see the job progress, they tend to realize they overlooked some considerations or feel differently about changes such as upgrades, reconfigurations, and add-ons.

How you, the landlord, and the contractor handle these items depends on who is in charge of construction and who you have hired to help you. In general, you are responsible for the majority of changes that lead to cost overruns. When it is apparent there will be a cost overrun, the savvy landlord will require you to contribute your share of the overage first, and the landlord will pay their portion next. This ensures that the landlord will not end up with an unfinished construction site in the event you unexpectedly cannot pay your portion. Landlords will do everything they can to avoid this outcome.

I have found the best result for clients is usually created by working with a landlord who is used to providing tenant improvements on a turnkey basis. The turnkey concept is that the landlord is in charge of design, funding, and construction. They deliver a completed space you can move in to, and you can be up and running in the least amount of time possible. You can leverage their skillset so you stay focused on what you do best, rather than dipping your toe into the construction industry. The landlords who will be open to this are usually the landlords who own portfolios of property and are used to working with contractors on a daily basis.

NEXT STEPS

In this chapter, we discussed considerations for the office portion of the building, which is what most people think of when they envision construction. However, the warehouse portion of your property usually covers a considerable amount of square footage and has its own unique considerations, which will we examine in the next chapter.

CHAPTER 10

WAREHOUSE OPTIMIZATION

While the office is often an executive's focus because that is where most of the company employees spend their time, the warehouse is the heart of any industrial business. Warehouses are almost always in shell condition, and the tenant is responsible for the vast majority of construction, installation, and improvement. Your racking, machinery, and electrical distribution are specific to your business and generally not reusable by a future tenant. In most cases, landlords will not foot the bill here. Landlords will sometimes participate in upgrading roll-up doors, dock equipment, and sprinkler systems that have a useful life beyond your initial lease. Since you are primarily in charge of outfitting your warehouse, it pays to be prudent.

PRODUCTION MACHINES

A manufacturing operation consists of machines and equipment that workers use to create finished goods. Manufacturing can be automotive, aerospace, industrial supply, apparel, food (which we will discuss separately later in this chapter), plastic mold injection, medical devices, and more. All manufacturing industries need to bring in raw materials, then process, assemble, package, store, and distribute their goods. They also have machines that require footings, installation, calibration, certification, and wiring.

Before installing machinery, you need a precise warehouse layout design showing where each machine will be. I have seen companies move their machinery several times while they expanded and reworked their process. I have also seen aerospace manufacturers not touch a thing for twenty years. I always tell my clients Bob Barry's mantra of "improve while you move": every time you relocate your warehouse, you can improve your process and invest in your future.

Slab thickness is vital for manufacturing. It is important to know what kind of slab you have, its age, its thickness, and potentially the soil conditions underneath the slab. Larger stamps, presses, and printing machines require pouring footers and thicker concrete pads, replacing the standard concrete slab to provide an adequate foundation for heavy machinery.

After being moved, many machines will require calibration and certification. This calibration and certification takes time and talent, and an experienced project manager and industrial engineer can help you navigate this process.

ELECTRICITY

The most common electrical work needed for industrial buildings has to do with machinery, equipment, forklifts, and office workstations. The main issues are the number of amps, type of voltage, distribution of electricity, backup generators, and transfer switches.

Electricity is one of the facets of industrial real estate that is most commonly misunderstood. Try asking ten team members the difference between 120/208 and 277/480 volts. Nine people will probably think you are speaking a foreign language, but there is usually one facility manager or engineer who understands electricity better than your electrician.

Amperage is the quantity of electricity available within the building. The most common question you will ask your broker, your team, and the landlord is "Does this building have enough power for my business?" You will need to hire a commercial electrician early in the process, because this is not considered the landlord's responsibility. The tenant is in charge of making sure the electrical supply is adequate, because it is specific to the tenant's business needs. Your first step is to create or update a spreadsheet that shows all of your machines' electrical requirements. You can then have an intelligent discussion about what your usage looks like under expected operating conditions.

A shortage of power can kill a deal because the cost of upgrading power to the building is usually cost-prohibitive: in Southern California, it can cost $10,000 to upgrade the power in the smallest of the small warehouses and more than $200,000 for medium and large warehouses. But as the size of the building increases and the lease term gets longer, the relative price of an electrical upgrade decreases, and the prospect of adding power increases.

Bringing more power to the building is a question for the local electrical utility. Getting the utility involved means you are entering their bureaucracy. Power can enter the property overhead or underground. Underground power lines are great for the image of the property, but they can make it harder to add electricity to a building. In many cases, the power runs through the ground near the sidewalk and street, which means the electrical utility often cannot access the electrical lines unless it cuts the asphalt from the road, the concrete of the walkway, the parking lot, and the building.

After digging, workers must install the electric conduit, fill in the trenches, and restore the exterior surfaces and landscaping. Then the inside of the property will need new breaker boxes, panels, subpanels, fuses, switches, and conduits.

Bob Barry of JBA says it is important for companies in this situation to look far down the road. "When you go into a building, you might have a beautiful building you get very excited about, but it may have 600 or 800 amps, and you may need 1200, or even more. The power requirements are both potentially a cost issue and a timeline issue, because then the power departments—whether in San Diego, Orange County, or LA—have a tough timeline. It is awesome if they have a year or more to complete an upgrade, but sometimes it does not work out that way."

BACKUP GENERATORS

Backup generators can prevent downtime and disruption in the event of power failure. Most businesses have them to satisfy industry regulations and licensing, although some have them simply to protect themselves.

Backup generators are gasoline-powered engines that switch on when the building electricity goes off. They can cost thousands to hundreds of thousands of dollars, depending on their size. It is generally cost-prohibitive to connect your whole building to your backup generator. Instead, prioritize by consulting the preliminary needs list you made of all of the power requirements of your existing machines and equipment. Separate the essential from the nonessential, understanding that your decisions will have design and cost implications.

Everything that needs to be connected must have its own dedicated outlet. This applies to lab equipment within climate-controlled areas, as well as machinery and HVAC systems. You have to decide if you really need your HVAC system to be backed up, whether it is practical, and/or whether you will have to design a new system. Some flex and R&D buildings, for example, have one large, shared HVAC system that cannot be readily separated or backed up in a cost-effective manner.

The generator's location is your next practical consideration. It must be close to the power panels, and it will need a foundation and possibly an enclosure. Most companies place a backup generator outside the back of the warehouse, near the trash enclosure.

The second-most-common location for a backup generator is on the side of the building in what was once a landscaped area, in which case you will need to think about rerouting water supply and drainage, and then pouring a pad and possibly an enclosure. The foundation dimensions can be six feet by six feet to upward of ten feet by ten feet, so it is helpful to have that in mind when you are looking at the back and side of the building. Some buildings only have three-foot or four-foot width of landscaping from the building's tilt-wall panel to the curb. Others do not have any room because they have a shared drive aisle, tight truck loading area, or no landscaping. When looking at the back of the building, you want to look at the grade-level and dock-high loading doors. This is to make sure the backup generator will not impede access and/or get in the way of your trucks or your neighbors.

The third-most-common place for a backup generator is in the parking lot. Taking a parking stall away from the parking lot may not be an issue, but in this case, you will need to trench through the parking lot, and you will have a longer length of concrete and asphalt to travel to get to the power panel.

Some cities will not require an enclosure, while others will mandate it and cite you for code enforcement issues if you do not have one. The more modern and newer the industrial neighborhood, the more likely it is the city requires an enclosure. It is always worth taking this into consideration up front to minimize expense and maximize utility. No pun intended.

The size, type, installation, and location of your backup generator are likely to have implications that total hundreds of thousands of dollars, so it pays to have a thorough and intelligent conversation with your project team about this.

FIRE SUPPRESSION

Fire suppression is a lump-sum category for all of the ways in which building fire and life safety systems work to prevent fires, give employees time to evacuate, and extinguish flames. Warehouses have different considerations than office space because they hold fewer people, have more cubic volume, and have different types of potentially flammable materials. At a minimum, your strategy should take into consideration the materials you are storing, how high you plan to store them, what kind of racking system you plan on using, the building's existing fire suppression system, and exit doors.

Fire suppression experts refer to what you store as your "commodity class." Each commodity class rating has different practical and financial implications. The higher the classification, the lower you must store your materials on your racking system and the higher the sprinkler rating requirements. Some classifications only allow for floor stacking.

The following are the fire authority's commodity classifications:

- Class I commodities include noncombustibles.
- Class II commodities include crates and boxes made of wood, and cardboard cartons.
- Class III commodities include wood, paper, and natural-fiber products.
- Class IV commodities include Group A plastics, which covers most types of consumer items, like toys, bottles, and home goods.
- Class V commodities include Group B plastics that are softer and more pliable, like tubing and nylon materials. Group C plastics like PVC and melamine plastics are also included. Plastic-specific concerns revolve around how hard they are to ignite, the chemicals released when burned, and the speed at which they burn.

Sometimes the classification process is simple. When a company specializes in a limited number of products and stores them in a uniform manner, the fire authority can simply classify these commodities and compare them to the warehouse's fire suppression system.

In other cases, the process is complicated. Take, for example, PODS, the portable storage containers used for residential moving. The PODS company may have hundreds of these units in their warehouse. One POD might have ten surfboards, whereas another might have two double beds and a couch. PODS are frequently packed with TVs, mattresses, and couches, which happen to be among the most concerning of flammable items to fire authorities. You can imagine how difficult it would be for a fire marshal to classify the PODS warehouse. Fire marshals are becoming increasingly more conservative and are sorting them into higher commodity classes by default.

When it comes to fire sprinklers, most experts will tell you to look at the fire riser first, the big red pipe in the back inside wall of the warehouse, and look for the sprinkler calculations on the silver tag. Sprinkler calculations will give you a gallon per minute numerator over a square footage denominator. Standard calculations are "unrated" for older systems: .45/2,500, .66/3,000, and ESFR, which stands for early suppression, fast response. A certain amount of water flows out of the sprinkler heads to disperse water over a specific size diameter of square feet, but it is not uncommon to find that there is no recognizable sprinkler calculation present. The system might predate the rating system, the tag may have fallen off, the rating may be illegible, or someone may have painted over it.

Less commonly known factors that can play a pivotal role in your ability to operate your business are the thickness of the water lines, the sprinkler water pipe pattern, the water pressure coming into the building, and the quantity and location of the fire riser(s).

If you have a mismatch between your commodity class and the existing fire suppression system in a building you are considering leasing, you have a few choices as to how to rectify the situation:

1. You can negotiate with the landlord for a fire sprinkler system upgrade. Your company might need the update to do business today, but it is the landlord's building, and it will be better equipped to lease to future companies like yours.
2. You can fund your own fire sprinkler upgrade depending on its value to your company and the expense of the upgrade.
3. You can speak with your material handling vendor and see if there is a different way to arrange your inventory to comply with the existing building conditions. Sometimes, in-rack sprinklers can provide a solution without needing a full building upgrade.

Each fire sprinkler upgrade is unique. It may involve replacing the sprinkler heads, replacing the sprinkler pipes with thicker-gauge pipes, changing the pipe pattern from branch line to grid pattern, and/or installing a pump to increase the water pressure. This is not cheap: on a 100,000-square-foot industrial building in Orange County, California, the total cost would typically range between $250,000 and $300,000.

Check on all of this information before you lease the building, because the best time to perform this upgrade is before you move in. It is possible to perform this upgrade in sections of the building after moving in, but this is less than ideal. The size of the sections in a phased installation depends on how many risers there are, how the existing system is set up, and the new system design.

If you do not know what kind of system you have, there are no markings on the fire riser, and there are no plans for the building, you are not the first to be in this situation. Incomplete information is more common than you might think, mostly because buildings have different owners over time, each owner has different tenants, and rarely are all of the plans transferred between these parties.

In this case, first try calling the city and asking them for any building plans, including sprinkler design and calculations. Expect to encounter a wide variety of records. Some cities have high-quality digital files, while others have old microfiche systems, and some cities do not have any building plans, due to floods or fires. In the event of the worst-case scenario, you can hire a fire sprinkler engineer to test the system and calculate the sprinkler's capabilities.

You may also want to consider if there are older existing fire curtains within the building that can or need to be removed and the regulations for the distance and path of travel for fire exits. I have found that if you take an older manufacturing building and try to upgrade its fire systems to suit distribution needs, there may be more considerations than normal.

Here is where it pays to have material handling and high-pile permit experts to guide you. High-pile permit consultants are part of a cottage industry: ex-firefighters who provide consulting for companies and help them obtain high-pile permits. The reason that ex-firefighters are in this industry is because they used to perform the inspections and deal with the city, but from the other side of the counter. Their specialty is assisting companies in classifying their commodity class, ensuring their existing warehouse sprinkler system is sufficient to store goods above twelve feet, and securing the high-pile permits necessary to get the company's certificate of occupancy from the city. I have found they are worth hiring in complex, high-value, and time sensitive projects.

DOCK EQUIPMENT

Chances are there will be some changing of the dock equipment during the lease of a new building or during a lease extension on an existing building. There are always improvements to be made, operational factors to consider, and plain old wear and tear to deal with. In our discussion of dock equipment, we will include bumpers, levelers, plates, and ramps.

At a minimum for dock equipment, you need a rubber dock bumper that will keep your trailer or container from physically hitting the concrete dock or tilt-wall panel when it is being backed up into the loading area. Bumpers come in different shapes and sizes. The negotiation of a lease is the perfect time to have the landlord replace any bumpers that are past their useful life.

Dock levelers, plates, and ramps are the next three workhorses that bridge the gap between the container and the warehouse floor. The pallet jack and forklift will have to drive over these into the container to pick up the pallet, reverse back into the warehouse speed bay, and move onward to their next destination. It is essential to make this path of travel safe and efficient.

Dock levelers are the most permanent and heavy-duty solution commonly employed in industrial real estate. The three main types of dock levelers are hydraulic, mechanical, and "edge-of-dock" levelers. The type of material being loaded, its weight, and its packaging will usually dictate what size levelers you require, and the flow of your operation will dictate the quantity and location of these levelers. It is important to know this in advance, as each one costs thousands of dollars.

You cannot assume that new buildings have dock levelers. When you are the first company to occupy a building in a ground-up development, it is common for the developer to include some dock levelers, but they are not sufficient for the needs of most companies. It is important to go into negotiations knowing what type, size, and brand of dock leveler you require and to create enough leverage in the negotiation to have them included within your landlord's tenant improvement package. I was able to do this while negotiating a lease on 80,000 square feet of distribution space in a new industrial park in San Antonio, Texas, next to Amazon. Our attention to this detail meant that while the landlord was building out our office space, they were also demolishing parts of the dock area and digging the pits to house the leveler hydraulics.

Edge-of-dock levelers are very short and wide steel plates with a hinge that lifts manually to bridge the gap between a container and the dock's edge. It is useful to test each edge-of-dock leveler during the first thirty days of the lease to ensure each one works, as they can still be a few thousand dollars to replace. I have worked with a national flooring distributor for the last ten years, on over 200,000 square feet of warehouse space. One of the buildings we leased had new edge-of-dock levelers installed. Upon further investigation, we found that some of the welds were faulty, leading to an unsafe environment where the leveler could snap under heavy loads. Fortunately, we discovered this before it caused an accident. However, the landlord thought it was our fault and we had damaged the leveler. We had to find a competing dock installer to inspect the docks and prove it was, in fact, a faulty installation before the landlord decided to do the right thing and replace it for us.

Dock plates are mobile pieces of corrugated steel that are set down between a container and the dock door. These dock plates are practical for small deliveries loaded and unloaded by hand, as opposed to by forklift. They are cheap to acquire and easy to use, but also easily damaged. They do not require installation and are typically used to deal with less-than-ideal loading situations.

The purpose of a truck ramp is to connect the inside of the warehouse to the loading area outside, where the docks are located, when distribution buildings do not have grade-level loading. With this challenge, there are two common remedies. The safest, yet more costly option: pour concrete to create a permanent ramp. The more cost-effective and portable option: bolt a steel ramp to the ground. This ramp can be moved to different positions or removed and resold later. I have found that landlords will sometimes contribute toward the installation of concrete ramps because they are considered an improvement to the property, whereas a steel ramp is the tenant's personal property and can go with them wherever they move. Concrete ramps should be installed at the same time as dock levelers before you move in.

Lastly, measure the distance between the ground and the loading dock. On the odd occasion, a loading dock or truck well height can be a few inches higher or lower than normal. This is a surprising issue I have run into a handful of times. It is not a good feeling when you back up your first truck to the docks to deliver the first shipment into your brand-new building, only to find out you have a problem.

FENCING

If you want to install exterior fencing to protect your trucks, equipment, trailers, or shipping containers, you should do so while you are doing construction on your office and warehouse. Most fencing is relatively standard wrought iron or chain link.

I have found that sometimes you need to rework existing fencing as well. In one instance, I sold a 46,000-square-foot building to a health food supplement company in Costa Mesa, California. We were in escrow with a credible buyer when everything came screeching to a halt. The buyer had reviewed their property survey and realized a part of the fencing did not go all the way out to the corner of the property. On the other side of the fence was the neighbor who had taken over that part of our property a decade earlier and had installed a picnic table and break area. Imagine our surprise when we learned a picnic table was creating such a large problem. We had to reach out to the neighbor, negotiate a solution for them to relocate their lunch area, and then hire a fencing company to relocate the fencing to the property line before the sale could be completed.

Learn from our experience: always double-check the property fencing line before you sign the lease.

SCALES

Scales are important for some logistics companies that have to weigh their truckloads, and these companies must install them on-site if there are not weighing stations conveniently located nearby. If this is the case, it is essential to find an industrial property with the right yard dimensions. If a fully loaded trailer is 74 feet and most truck courts average a minimum of 110 feet, you can see how important it is to map out traffic and make sure the warehouse can accommodate the scale position, along with all other company-related truck traffic.

You can install an above-ground or below-ground scale, but either way, you will need landlord approval. Landlords will want to know the make, model, and type of construction needed to install and remove the scale, and they may ask you to remove it when you leave the property.

If you run a company that utilizes scales for your trucking operation, be mindful that any property you find with a scale in place is not necessarily a good thing. Sometimes you will find the manufacturer no longer makes parts for old scales. They can actually be a liability in that you need to remove the old scale before installing your new one. I discovered this while helping a logistics client in Tampa, Florida. However, we were fortunate, and there was a public scale we could utilize nearby instead of replacing the old, dilapidated scale.

ROOF LIFTING

Roof lifting is a specialized kind of general contracting reserved for older, functionally obsolescent warehouses. We will focus on its use in industrial buildings here, but it also works for retail buildings and other commercial applications.

If you decide to lift the roof on your existing building, you save money on relocation expenses, tenant improvements, and project management. You also save on disruption of time and effort, and more. With roof lifting, the question is, how much will this process increase your capacity, and at what cost?

Here is an outline of the primary steps involved in roof lifting:

- The contractor supports the existing roof with hydraulics.

- All building systems connected from the tilt-wall panel to the roof are separated.
- The roof is separated from the four walls and columns.
- The roof is incrementally raised, using hydraulic lifts.
- New support columns are installed to support the higher ceiling clearance.
- The building systems are reconnected.
- The facade that raises the surrounding four walls is constructed.

In an interview with Toronto's premier roof lifter, Marty Shiff of Rooflifters, we discussed how the roof-lifting feasibility process begins as an exploratory mission. The general contractor walks the job site to understand the client's operational needs and inspect the property conditions. If the old roof was recently replaced and under a manufacturer's and installer's warranty, then the installer will be looped into the conversation. You will spend a few thousand dollars on preliminary engineering studies and drawings, along with concrete slab borings and initial pressure testing. Just like tenant improvements can be paid for and performed by the landlord or tenant, roof lifting can too.

Not all industrial buildings can have their roof lifted, though. The main limiting factor to explore during the feasibility process is if the concrete slab can sustain the increased load on the floor from the higher roof and subsequent fully loaded higher racking system. Additional feasibility is required for the existing fire suppression system, electricity, roof drains, and roof warranty.

One overlooked benefit to roof lifting is the speed of the project. A roof lifting project can take just a few months from inception to completion because, in most cases, roof lifting is allowable within a warehouse's current zoning code.

There are obvious concerns regarding safety, weather, and timing considerations. Given careful consideration and preparation, it is possible to lift the roof while occupying the warehouse with modest disruption, creating an immediate increase in capacity. From a practical standpoint, you may need to find temporary space for your inventory in order to accommodate the breakdown and removal of the existing racking system, and then the installation, inspection, and loading of your new racking.

It may not be necessary to lift the entire roof in some cases. Let us say you have manufacturing in one half of the building and distribution in the other half of the building. You have reorganized your production line and invested in new machinery to meet demand, contributing to higher inventory levels. In this case, you can raise the roof on half the building to accommodate higher racking without disrupting the manufacturing side of your operation.

SPECIALIZED USES

If you are in the food, beverage, and cold storage industry, or the life sciences industry, you face a number of additional considerations. We will focus on these here because they are the most prevalent in the industrial real estate market.

FOOD, BEVERAGE, AND COLD STORAGE

Food-related uses have unique regulations and industry standards with major real estate implications. The Safe Quality Food Institute (SQFI), the United States Department of Agriculture (USDA), and the United States Food and Drug Administration (FDA) are the primary regulatory food agencies ensuring food production companies adhere to strict health, safety, and accountability standards. The Food Safety Modernization Act (FSMA), enacted in 2011, has led to a need for modernizing the way food is grown, harvested, and processed.

I have advised executives of food companies that produce baked goods, bread, frozen yogurt, ice cream, smoothies, frozen fruits, frozen vegetables, soups, sauces, broths, and teas, as well as craft breweries and beer distributors. While each operation is different, there are similarities in their needs.

PROGRAMMING

Kate Lyle is one of Ware Malcomb's top architectural and design specialists for industrial cold storage, food, and beverage projects, and she is a resource for my clients. She articulates how programming can sometimes take much longer than anticipated in food production due to the abundance of intricacies involved. It can take months to years from project vision to construction, depending on how intensive the programming process is.

Kate helps clients determine whether it makes more sense to design a "box-in-box" system, or whether the whole building should be part of the refrigerated system. The first option is where the building shell is built, and there is a climate-controlled system within the building, whereas the second application uses the walls of the building and the roof insulation as the system. Each municipality has different codes that dictate which application they will allow; other internal considerations are important, like fire suppression systems, roof structure, and reusability concerns.

REUSABILITY

It is always a challenge to repurpose another company's food production building. In expensive coastal markets, it is cost-prohibitive to find suitable land, buy it, and build a custom food plant from scratch. In the Midwest, though, where there is greater land availability and lower cost of land and construction, build-to-suits are more commonplace. It is difficult to find industrial buildings used by a food producer that can now accommodate another food production company. This is because every company has their own proprietary methods and manufacturing processes. For example, making pretzel chips is a very different process than making hot sauce or Greek yogurt. It can be very difficult to find a match between an old location, size, temperature of cooler and freezer spaces, and your other requirements. The same goes for floor drains, clarifiers, and wash-down walls, which usually are not the right size, shape, or orientation to provide any real value. Other common issues include ceiling clearance height, room adjacencies for flow and thermal, or refrigeration efficiencies. Old food production buildings present an obstacle to most new food companies because it can cost six figures to remove all of the existing improvements before building out the new ones.

COOLER/FREEZER

As discussed above, the cooler and freezer application for existing retrofit facilities is commonly described as a "box in box." Think of it like a couple of Russian nesting dolls. The inside box is the climate-controlled space; it has its own four walls and ceiling and is built within the larger box of the warehouse.

For cold storage and freezer-driven companies, new construction can be beneficial so the underfloor heating and insulation can be installed. It is possible to do this when retrofitting an existing building, but it can be expensive. In retrofits, concrete is only removed and replaced in the freezer section of the building, for installation of the heating and insulation elements. This might be less important for broadline foodservice distributors with tri-temperature warehouses to handle products that need to be chilled or frozen or need ambient climates.

There are a variety of different cooler and freezer systems and applications that have changed over time, so you should be conservative if you are trying to work with any existing system. I routinely bring in several specialized architecture, construction, and industrial engineers to help identify the condition of existing buildings and assess the potential for a successful retrofit.

COLD-READY SPECULATIVE CONSTRUCTION

Kate Lyle also explains how she has helped developers design the cold storage speculative construction design of the future. As e-commerce effects have rippled throughout the food and beverage industry, so has capital, and industrial developers are now interested in building cold storage on a speculative basis, thanks to innovative architects like Kate and Ware Malcomb. The cost of a cold storage building can be upward of three times that of a regular dry building. Kate and her team have designed ways to improve the building envelope so it has all the right building characteristics for users, who can then customize their own thermal envelope at a price a developer can afford.

It is this new cold-ready speculative development that can provide new opportunity for executives to open a new warehouse without going through the costly and challenging process of converting a dry warehouse to a cold one.

INCREASED ACCESS CONTROL

This type of building will most often include a lobby area where visitors need to sign in and put on proper attire before they enter the rest of the facility. Most companies require a hair net at minimum; some require a smock, beard net, safety glasses, hard hat, and booties to cover shoes. Thick insulated jackets for going into cooler and freezer rooms may also be required.

INCREASED WORKER DENSITY AND INTENSITY

An increased number of production workers per shift and quantity of shifts results in the need for additional warehouse restrooms with higher stall counts, larger break rooms, locker rooms, and more parking. Special supply air requirements are needed for production spaces to finely balance the air pressures between adjacent spaces. With an increased production schedule, in some instances, manufacturers run three shifts, twenty-four hours a day, seven days a week. The transitions between shifts can oftentimes be when creative parking arrangements are necessary.

ENERGY SUPPLY AND DISTRIBUTION

Utilities and energy availability are vital for this industry. It usually requires machines that blend, mix, convey, and package. Food and beverage production requires cooler and freezer space, conveyor systems, blast freezers, and spiral freezers in many applications. All of these require more energy than dry systems, and this energy needs to be distributed throughout the warehouse with additional subpanels, transformers, switches, and backup generators. Cold storage requires additional refrigeration units, and there are different types of systems to consider. Ammonia systems were prevalent for a long period of time, whereas freon systems are now commonly used on applications under 125,000 square feet. Carbon dioxide refrigeration systems are also now more widely used. Examine whether or not utilities are regulated, as this needs to be factored into your real estate project as well.

OUTDOOR STORAGE AND TRUCKING CONSIDERATIONS

Many companies need to store ingredients such as sugar, oil, and flour in large silos outside of their building. These silos and tanks require concrete footings. They usually do not require screening or enclosures, but they do require coring through the tilt-wall panel for pipes to connect them to the building. All of these installations will need to be removed and patched when the lease expires.

Additionally, in some cities, refrigerated trucks are not allowed to be within a certain distance of residential developments. You will want to verify this with the local city zoning department as part of your due diligence.

MEZZANINE

Some food production warehouses install steel platforms, or mezzanines, within the warehouse building to create a second story. This second story can be used for office space or for welfare space above process areas with low ceilings. Commercial general contractors install these mezzanines and will require concrete footings. Mezzanines are not unique to food production: they are also used in high-velocity distribution, aerospace, and engineering.

Mezzanines can be expensive to install and remove, and this

can cause a major real estate dispute. One of my partners and I represented a private family who had sold their food production company to a large conglomerate, and years later the conglomerate decided to sell the building. That sale produced considerable litigation over the mezzanine. The tenant thought the mezzanine was part of the building because it had footings connecting the steel beams to the foundation. In contrast, the landlord and seller believed the mezzanine was a trade fixture, to be removed at the end of the lease obligation. The mezzanine cost a few hundred thousand dollars to remove, so it was something both parties had a vested interest in settling. The lesson learned was that when building a mezzanine within a leased property, it is vital to consider the impact of this improvement during the initial lease negotiation phase and to have a clear understanding of your restoration responsibilities.

WATER SUPPLY, CLARIFIERS, WATER DISCHARGE

Depending on the type of food production, it is common for buildings to need a more abundant supply of water. Water supply depends on water pressure and the size of the water line coming from the city water supply.

Water and ensuing liquid waste can require different types of separators and clarifiers. These work like they are panning for gold: different-sized screens will screen out waste particulates. Clarifiers can also require approval and credits from the city, and only a certain amount of waste can go through the system at one time.

Food producers must be aware of their wastewater needs so they can grow in areas that accommodate their discharge needs. Many large companies have spent considerable resources exploring industrial property developments, only to find out late in the negotiations that the locale cannot accommodate their discharge requirements.

LOADING

Many operations require temperature-controlled dock areas. Docks also need to be closed to outside elements with seals, shelters, screens, and motorized roll-up doors to keep out dust, dirt, bugs, and pests. Sometimes we can negotiate these into the tenant improvement allowance from the landlord.

Most food producers benefit by selecting an industrial building with a cross-dock orientation so raw materials can come into the building, and finished product can go out the other end. This cross-dock orientation is typically found on newer buildings. Older, traditional industrial buildings are usually oriented so all ingoing and outgoing materials go through the same loading area.

LIFE SCIENCES

The life sciences industry is expanding rapidly. Many companies are locating in clusters within geographic areas surrounding top research universities, like Boston, Seattle, San Jose, San Diego, and Orange County. Life science companies may specialize in research and development, pharmaceuticals, diagnostics laboratories, medical devices, and more. The following are some considerations unique to this industry.

Longer Lead Time

Timing can be critical for life science companies when relocating into a new, larger building. Regulatory notification, licensing, and inspections need to occur before, during, and after construction. It can make sense for life science companies to build out, move in to, and begin operating their new facility before closing down their old facility. Creating a new space is expensive because it may require buying all-new furniture, equipment, and supplies. This is in addition to their existing operation, so they can move from one building to another without downtime and disruption.

Life science companies also need to utilize climate-controlled moving companies to ensure their live tissues, blood samples, and cultures are all appropriately handled. They need to be maintained at regulated temperatures, and backup measures need to be in place.

Specialized Space Use

Life science companies also consider building image, parking availability, office build-out, and HVAC supply when considering relocation into a new industrial property. Having an architect with life science experience is critical. There are so many nuances to the interior lab space that a generalist will not be able to do the project and client justice.

Some improvements that life science companies may need are clean rooms, individual lab rooms, larger testing space with multiple lab benches, wet lab space, HEPA-air-filtered space, negative pressure rooms, assembly space, and testing space. These different types of climate-controlled areas include higher-end and more costly office materials.

Fume Hoods

Fume hoods require the ability to penetrate the roof membrane to provide for adequate venting and air circulation. Anytime you have to penetrate the roof, you need the landlord's permission. If the roof is less than ten years old, you may have to work with the landlord's roofer to work on the roof without voiding any kind of manufacturer and installer warranty. Landlords and tenants alike want to make sure that the roof is watertight, and as such, you will need proper prior approval before penetrating the roof, installing the hood ventilation, and patching around the penetration to ensure a watertight membrane.

R&D Properties

In the industrial real estate world, we have a subcategory of industrial property known as "flex," "flex-tech," or "research and development" (R&D) that is very prevalent and sought-after in the life science community. This subcategory is most often a concrete tilt-up building with more refined exterior architecture and more abundant parking. The higher parking ratio supports a larger office build-out and corresponding employee count. The property includes a robust HVAC system and a combination of rooftop units to supply climate-controlled space through the vast majority of the building.

R&D properties will often have two-story offices based on the construction type. As a result, landlords and investors can sometimes repurpose two-story office buildings into R&D buildings by installing roll-up doors and grade-level loading. This gives landlords the flexibility to lease the space to either an R&D tenant, a traditional office tenant, a coworking tenant, or a creative office tenant.

Opaque Leasing Market

Appraisers have a difficult time appraising these properties because it is hard to find accurate and comparable leasing information.

First, this is because R&D properties are rare: they do not exist in many markets with traditional warehouse industries. Second, and more importantly, R&D properties are unique. They may exist on industrial, office, medical, or research and development zoned land. They may look like a warehouse or a corporate office. They may have an office that looks high-end but has roll-up doors in the back.

It pays to have a broker who is experienced in R&D industrial property. One of my colleagues handled a lease renewal for an aerospace company that was leasing a 150,000-square-foot building with 60 percent office, 40 percent assembly space, and four hundred employees. During negotiations, the tenant tried to use the lower industrial property lease rates to advocate for why their extension should be affordable. The landlord tried to increase the lease rate by using low-rise office space comparables. Because each party took such an extreme position, they went through a nasty, expensive, and distracting litigation to determine fair market value. This type of ambiguity can be avoided by working with a broker who has a track record of success in these types of transactions.

PROJECT COMPLETION

It is time to set the stage to move in to your new building—it is time to orchestrate the actual move. A careful transition from one building to another will be felt and experienced by your company in positive ways. In the next chapter, we will cover how to get to the moment when everyone settles into the new building. There is nothing like walking into a new building for the first time and experiencing the mindset shift where everything new is possible.

CHAPTER 11

TRANSITIONING SEAMLESSLY

The start of the moving process is the most tangible part of the process for people because it is literally when every single person in your company is involved. There is a lot leading up to the actual day of the move. A project manager will have a detailed checklist that incorporates various considerations. My job here is to give you an overview to help you know what to expect if you choose to manage your own relocation, and to help set expectations.

FURNITURE, FIXTURES, AND EQUIPMENT

In your lease document and within the industry, we call everything you bring into the property "furniture, fixtures, and equipment" (FF&E). Before you can think about moving out of your current property to the new one, the new property must be functional and ready to receive your FF&E. Here is how you can prepare your IT, furniture, and equipment for moving day.

IT

In the last decade, cloud-based infrastructure has replaced most on-site servers in offices. However, there is usually a need for on-site server space for internal networks, wireless routers, copiers, printers, and audiovisual, at a minimum. Additional IT-related considerations revolve around workplace sensors, smart appliances, and the warehouse. The warehouse of yesterday involved racking and forklifts, but the modern warehouse and the warehouse of the future include automation and robotics systems that have their own IT and electrical needs.

Internal IT departments of companies, third-party IT consultants, and internet service providers usually need extra time to properly budget, coordinate, and execute their parts of the system setup. IT departments usually require multiple stakeholder approvals for equipment purchases and vendor agreements, which can take months of additional time. For example, one IT contract for new equipment procurement might need internal IT approval, finance approval, legal review, and executive approval before it can be fully implemented. Then the equipment needs to be ordered, received, and installed. Then employees may require training. The concept of improving your operation while you move also means you might have new methods to learn during the process. Giving this careful consideration in advance can help you avoid any turmoil.

Add to these considerations the fact that any new warehouse automation and robotics initiative will have a considerable IT component to it. This is because automation systems must be integrated within your internal ERP system. The warehouse must be mapped so any automation system can identify where all building systems and products are located, along with adjustments and refinements along the way.

FURNITURE

Many tenants believe they can have their mover break down their furniture, transport it, and then reassemble it in their new space with minimal adjustments overnight. Rarely is this the reality. Any major relocation will inevitably include a rearranging of office personnel to fit into the new space. Architects and furniture vendors excel at this task and will save you multiple headaches.

Trying to time the completion of construction, the receipt and installation of furniture, IT, the relocation crew, and the start of rent payments can be daunting even for professionals. Without professionals, the room for error is rather large. You do not want your new furniture delivered too early, while contractors are in the building, and you do not want the furniture delivered too late, when you are rushing to meet deadlines, so timely scheduling is essential. Your mover can usually be a lifeline for you in that they can hold furniture within their warehouse until the building is ready to receive it.

Installation can take multiple days, and even weeks in larger offices. During this time, you may find unforeseen surprises that require adjustment. For instance, you might find that too many desks are located in an area with unacceptable sun glare or that all of the glass offices are aesthetically attractive but require additional sound dampening and privacy screening.

Let us not forget about the artwork. Some people overlook decor, while others have full-blown murals that cover entire walls within their space. What you choose depends on the people in your organization and what speaks to the company culture. You will want all artwork installed after the furniture installation, but oftentimes before your contractor punch list, depending on how invasive the artwork installation process is.

EQUIPMENT-MOVING CONCERNS

In the warehouse, relocation specialists can help you move racking, forklifts, machines, and lab equipment. Their work can also include dismantling, crating, loading, transporting, and installing machinery.

Machines can require moving techniques from specialized "machine movers," otherwise known as "riggers." The most prevalent concerns involve machines that require precision calibration, Underwriters Laboratories safety certification, concrete footings, mezzanine installation, and temperature control.

Machinery moving and rigging is a cottage industry, so there are usually only a handful of options in each area. Whom you decide to work with depends on the size and complexity of your operation and geographic distance of the move.

Refer to the following lists for steps that should occur throughout the moving process.

+/- 90 Days Out

- Interview moving companies. Each one has its own method of bidding, much like the general contractors we discussed in the tenant improvement chapter. Make sure your moving bids are comparable, and use each bid to help clarify the others.
- Bid out your machinery moving to multiple specialized movers. You will find there will be little overlap in service between a traditional mover and a heavy machinery mover. This can be yet another area that will bring forth clarity and competition. Consider whether your machines or equipment have warranties, and if those warranties require specific vendors.

- Inventory all of your furniture and equipment, and the contents of your offices and warehouse. Note which pieces have special needs for disassembly, reassembly, and care during moving.
- Evaluate your mover's insurance policies, waivers, and disclaimers. Your contract with your mover is like your contract with your landlord and your contractor. It pays to be crystal clear on who is responsible for what, and what happens when people deviate from the agreed-upon job. You may want to have your attorney review this contract.
- Check with your existing and new landlord to see if they require a copy of your insurance certificate.
- Discuss security procedures and access with movers, vendors, and employees, especially if the move will take multiple days. It is imperative to clarify who is allowed at the job site and how building security will work.

+/- 60 Days Out

- Develop a strategy for communications to all employees, as well as a migration plan mapping out the department's timing and location.
- Plan the closing, redirection, and setup of services like mail, phones, faxes, and telecom services.
- Update vendors for supplies like water delivery, coffee service, and office supplies.
- Notify and update service agreements, licenses, insurance, and equipment leases with your new address and the timing of the move.
- Have your marketing department update all marketing collateral and order any new physical materials that require a new address, such as brochures, placards, letterhead, envelopes, and business cards.

- Plan announcements, schedule an open house, and send out press releases.
- Confirm the setup and installation of all operating systems in the new building, like water, power, elevators, emergency phone, HVAC units, and fire and life safety systems.
- Contact your moving company to confirm the numbers of totes, cartons, and containers needed. Schedule the distribution of all packing equipment.

+/- 30 Days Out

- Schedule the delivery and installation of new furniture and equipment.
- Explain to each employee what they will be required to do. For instance, remove the contents from their desks, pack their books and files, and color-code their boxes.
- Develop a color-coded floor plan of the new facility to show where to place all items.
- Color code all furniture and equipment.
- Tape keys to empty desks and file cabinets. Make sure you have duplicate keys.
- Install locks at new facilities and make duplicate keys. Distribute keys to appropriate team members.
- Arrange for the distribution of parking passes and security cards for the new facility. Maintain proper records for control and audit procedures.
- Schedule staff for unpacking and stocking supply cabinets, storerooms, and file rooms. Remove tags from all furniture and equipment to ensure you are operational as soon as possible.
- Prepare an employee welcome packet for the new space (including areas such as restrooms, gyms, break rooms, and copy rooms).

- Create a list of emergency contacts, cell phone numbers, and vendors for your project team that includes the moving company, building management, utilities, and telecommunications.
- Arrange for the old facility to be cleaned after the move has been completed.

+/- 7 Days Out

- Put up directional signs, room and area labels, and furniture plans in the new facility.
- Distribute contact lists for emergency/on-site/on-call lists.
- Create a "lost and found" department to locate lost boxes, personal items, and so on.
- Back up computer systems.
- Protect elevator cabs, lobbies, walls, and floors against damage from moving.
- Confirm transfer of your certificate of insurance from the insurance company.

Move-In Day

- Check inventory as contents load into each moving van.
- Walk the perimeter to look into elevators, lobbies, hallways, and offices before the last moving truck leaves to check for any items that have been left behind.
- Record the time the mover arrives and the number of movers working on your move.
- Carefully read the bill of lading before you sign it. The bill of lading is the document that serves as an inventory for your goods as they are loaded onto the truck and provides pertinent details of the move like the location, pricing, and delivery dates. Keep it with you until everything is delivered, charges are paid, and any claims are settled.

- Indicate any damaged boxes or items on the mover's inventory before signing paperwork.
- Distribute employee welcome packets.
- Coordinate with IT and electricians to be on hand for moving day to handle real-time troubleshooting and requests.

Post-move

- Distribute a new contact list and a map of department locations.
- Reconfirm the termination of old leases and the return of security deposits.
- Confirm the proper completion, delivery, and installation of all items on both the construction and vendor punch lists.
- Connect with maintenance vendors for the new facility's operating systems.
- Establish housekeeping rules.
- Audit final invoices against contract progress payments and pay retention.
- Complete and file all warranty information for new furniture and equipment.
- Update the fixed asset accounting system for any new furniture and equipment purchased. Do not forget to delete old furniture and equipment sold or given to charity.
- Confirm the change-of-address corrections.
- Update address for business certificates, the State Board of Equalization, and the certificate of occupancy.

SURRENDER, RESTORATION, DECOMMISSIONING

Most people take a nostalgic moment to look back at the old warehouse, think about how the company grew over time, and memorialize all of the moments that made their company what it is today. After that moment, it is vital to read through your lease one last time, specifically the section labeled Surrender, because it describes the condition in which you must deliver the property back to the landlord.

Any sophisticated landlord will ask you to remove your old network cabling. If the tenant leaves cabling behind, it will become the obligation and expense of the landlord to remove it. New tenants do not want to be responsible for removing the existing network cablings if they are outdated and unusable. Do not disregard this part of the lease, or you might be surprised when cabling removal expenses are deducted from your security deposit.

In the warehouse, the most commonly overlooked decommissioned item is the repair of the concrete slab. It is mandated by code for anchor bolts to secure your racking down to the concrete slab at specific torque levels, especially in areas of seismic activity. When racking is removed, these bolts need to be clipped and ground down before the remaining divot in the concrete is filled in with epoxy and smoothed. The result will be a floor in similar condition to when you first leased the building. This process may not sound like a big deal until you imagine the reality of four thousand bolts that need clipping, grinding, filling, and smoothing. Heavy-duty machines installed on footers can damage the concrete slab during operation, and disassembly and will need to be considered as well.

If you procure new racking and machines for your new building, you will need to assess what to do with the old racking and machinery. It is common to have the general manager designate someone to sell all of the old items. Auction houses can stage an auction on-site, or liquidators can remove everything for a flat fee. Decide what you need most: compensation, convenience, or cost avoidance.

We worked with a global supplier of industrial brake pads in Ontario, California, that was moving their manufacturing to Mexico and hired us to sell their existing 42,000-square-foot warehouse. They managed to sell half of the machinery and tools they no longer needed, but it took six months of countless meetings, haggling, pickups, and canceled appointments. While they recouped tens of thousands of dollars, it also took an enormous amount of the facility manager's time.

The Surrender section will have language regarding the repair and restoration of the building systems at the end of the lease. Since you took possession of the building with all of the systems in good working order, you should return the building with everything in good working order, with wear and tear excepted. This concept seems straightforward, but there is plenty of room for ambiguity.

For example, what if you were in the building for ten years, and when you initially signed the lease, the HVAC units were ten years old. Now these units are twenty years old, and they still work with regular service but are not as reliable as they once were. Depending on your lease, you may have an obligation to replace some of the units that are near the end of their useful life.

This same idea relates to the roof. Earlier, we discussed how not all triple net leases are created equal. The roof is one of the items that can change, depending on the kind of contract you have. Some people think the landlord should be responsible for the roof. It is their building, after all. Landlords often think the roof is the tenant's responsibility because of the nature of the triple net lease. But if you read through enough contracts, you will see there is no exact standard.

A great example of this happened with a global, publicly traded life science company we represent. We leased 100,000 square feet and added twenty HVAC units to the roof to support their laboratory operations. Some landlords want to keep all of these units at the end of the lease, thinking they add value to the property. Other landlords want these HVAC units removed so they do not have to pay to remove the units, as most companies that would lease the property next would not need them. We were able to negotiate within the lease for the tenant to leave the units at the end of the lease. Oftentimes, you will find this is a point of contention, and the landlord will usually ask for the option to decide at the end of the lease whether or not they want the tenant to remove their improvements.

When it comes to the parking lot, some companies can be harder on asphalt and concrete than others. Some trucking operations are notoriously tough on asphalt, trailer yards, and truck courts. Imagine hot summer days with fully loaded trucks making slow, tight turns on warm, sticky asphalt. Imagine storing trailers with trailer stands dug into the asphalt, day after day, for eighteen hundred days in a row. You may be responsible for replacing the entire parking lot, depending on the amount of damage. The acceptable solution may be two to three times more expensive than the simple slurry coat you may have in mind.

You will have to remove your sign from the top of the building and repair any damage done to the tilt-wall panel or facade once completed. Sometimes, you will be able to strike an arrangement with the landlord for your sign to go down at the same time the new tenant's goes up and use the same vendor. This simultaneous removal and installation is possible, but often hard to coordinate.

TIME TO CELEBRATE

Enjoy your open house, as it is a beautiful moment to celebrate a job well done for everyone on the relocation team and everyone in the company. I have seen some companies take this opportunity to invite folks from their corporate office, bring their spouses and kids to work, and offer fun team-building activities like raffles, dunk tanks, taco trucks, and more. The purpose of the celebration is to mark the successful completion of a resource-consuming and challenging project, and signal the time for new growth prospects to come. How will you celebrate your company's new location?

CHAPTER 12

ONGOING SUPPORT

I am a blue belt in Jiu-Jitsu, the powerful Brazilian martial art and combat sport. One of my favorite parts of the Jiu-Jitsu experience is that you line up in rank every day, with the most skilled grappler on one end and the new guy on the other. When it is time to train, everybody pairs up, and the most experienced person pairs with the least experienced person, and so on, all the way down the line. This way, every person has an opportunity to learn, work with peers, and teach. After you train in this manner for an hour, you get a chance to spar with people of all skill levels to test your knowledge and gain insights through practice.

At Gracie Barra, the gym where I have trained for years, I am blessed to train alongside a number of black belts who provide me with ongoing support. They can pinpoint exactly where I am in my journey to black belt within the first few minutes of sparring.

I am pleased to step into the role of experienced mentor whenever I speak with clients. Even if I have not talked to them in years, I can instantly understand where they are in a real estate process and help them right away. Like the Jiu-Jitsu black belts that help me, my real estate practice deliberately focuses on improving each aspect of helping clients, even after the lease contract is signed.

After the excitement of the move is over, I recommend that clients should debrief, abstract the lease, and consider lease administration. As time goes by, it pays to keep in touch with your landlord, integrate your real estate discussions into your quarterly management meetings, and make adjustments to your lease. I also help clients deal with surprises—some of which pop up with enough frequency that I can see them coming before the clients do.

PROJECT DEBRIEF

Your company has acquired its new industrial building, and your project team's job is complete. Great job, team! While all the details are fresh in your mind, you should memorialize the lessons learned in the process, as a lot can change over the first five to ten years you are in your warehouse.

Have each team member write down what worked, what did not, and what they wished they had known earlier. Then ask your assistant to compile these answers and identify trends in the feedback, key takeaways, and future actions. Transforming experience into learning is the process by which you build institutional capital your team can draw upon and use as raw material for continued growth.

LEASE ABSTRACT

A lease abstract is by far the most overlooked document in the history of commercial real estate. The abstract is a two-page brief of the lease document in Excel, with all the critical dates, dollars, rights, and obligations that you can upload into a database in the cloud. The purpose of a lease abstract is to have a form of the lease that is easy to access and manage, so you do not have to go through a sixty-page contract to solve a problem.

You will find your lease abstract helpful when the roof leaks and you are not sure who is responsible or whom to call. The same goes for HVAC, plumbing, lighting, dock equipment, and so on. Another great example is with subleases. When the roof leaks and you have subleased the building, you need to know if you should call your sublessor or the master lessor, now that three parties have some form of responsibility.

The most missed item is the option to extend your lease. As you reach the end of your lease, the landlord may be planning a huge rent increase, looking for a company with better credit who will sign a longer term than you will, or planning to sell the property to a user who will pay a higher price. If you exercise your option to renew and extend your lease, you have the right to be in the property for the foreseeable future and lease term. An option to extend the lease has to be exercised six, nine, or twelve months in advance of the lease expiration.

Executives usually do not have a system to remind them of dates like this, but you should, especially once you have multiple leases. You will want to systemize how you keep track of these dates. Most executives send their lease to their accounting department to pay the rent, and they do not look at it again. The accounting department will not look at it again until a problem arises. Even large and sophisticated companies miss dates due to lack of oversight or just because of the sheer volume of minutiae they have to tend to daily. Managing all these dates can be done simply, at a low cost. The industry term for this management is "lease administration."

Ask your broker to prepare a lease abstract for your new lease, or hire a third-party lease administration company to do it for you. The cost per abstract is nominal.

LEASE ADMINISTRATION

For companies with ten locations or more, lease administration software is the best way to keep track of all dates and dollars, rights and responsibilities, reconciliation, and option dates. Over the last ten years, we have seen the rise of property technology (PropTech) software. This gives us the ability to keep track of clients' leases within user-friendly databases on a per lease basis. The software rates are reasonable, and they come without a lot of the overhead or glut of features. A calendar overlays all real estate–related dates and provides teams with timely emails and alerts in advance of critical inflection points in the lease.

Many executives resist adding yet another type of software to manage, fearing it may not be worth the price and effort of implementation. I get it. If additional software is not for you, you can hire a third-party firm that specializes in lease administration. Most do an excellent job at this specialized work. Some brokerage houses have lease administration departments in-house as well, which will handle this for a monthly flat fee. Some provide the service free of charge if there are enough lease and sale transactions in your book of business to offset the cost.

BUSINESS PLANNING

If your company is anything like mine, you have quarterly and annual meetings where management tracks performance, reviews forecasts, and discusses high-level initiatives. At a minimum, your lease(s) should be addressed during your annual meeting. However, real estate–related matters are usually discussed quarterly and in board meetings, as real estate topics overlap with operations, finance, space use, HR, IT, and so on. This is so your company's vision can continue to align with your company's physical space. You do not want these to get out of alignment for long.

For example, if you are experiencing growth, you might try to increase the density of your office space to fit more employees before deciding to relocate. In the warehouse, the telltale sign is when you find yourself shuffling pallets because you cannot find enough space. Some companies even stack or stage steel shipping containers in the yard as an overflow measure before they decide they need more space.

I frequently see buildings reach their capacity of workers in the warehouse. This is most evident when a shift comes to an end and employees pour out into the parking lot, into the street, down the road, around the corner, and into vacant neighboring parking lots to be picked up by friends or family. Some manufacturing operations eventually find their parking shortage starts to impact their operations. One company I worked with had so many extra tractor-trailers during busy seasons, they stored them up and down the street and always received parking tickets and code enforcement notices during the holidays. Signs of overcapacity do not mean it is immediately time to move, but it is a signal you should be actively thinking about and discussing your future space needs.

In advance of annual and quarterly meetings, business leaders ask me to provide them with an analysis of their building in context of current market conditions. I will often offer a handful of different scenarios that provide multiple ways in which a current concern can be alleviated or approached in the future. These scenarios can be helpful for business leaders to provide context to their discussions about outside competitive forces, future legislative changes, and other internal business considerations.

For example, one trucking company I work with in South Florida noticed one of their competitors was going through a difficult point in their operation and was likely to close. This happened to coincide with my client's growth and our search for a suitable property. Their competitor had built a warehouse specifically with a trucking operation in mind, including unique characteristics that were not readily available in the industrial inventory. Because the client and I were working in lockstep and discussing these trends during our project, we were able to identify the opportunity, formulate a plan, and execute it. The result: we won the right to lease the building before it came to market.

Large tenants of industrial properties run operations that are capital-intensive. It takes time to formulate strategies and get executive buy-in, funding approval, and resource allocation. The more time you have to recognize trends and identify concerns, the more time you have to take ownership of your future and create opportunities that have a positive impact on your company's future growth potential.

LANDLORD COMMUNICATION

I have found it helpful to stay in touch with my clients' landlords each year as we make business adjustments. Industrial landlords commonly own property, buy land, and develop new buildings in multiple size ranges and geographic regions. Talk with your landlord about the other areas where you have business interests, and learn more about the direction of their investments. I have found local and national opportunities for clients that were off market, based purely on exploratory conversations with landlords.

BLEND AND EXTEND

Another ongoing way I support clients is by monitoring their lease rate compared to the market rate. At certain times in the market, we will find it is possible to lower the rent in exchange for an early lease renewal. In the industry, this is called a "blend and extend." In a descending market, tenants want rent relief because a descending market usually means decreasing revenue and GDP, and the need for lower overhead. On the other hand, landlords want occupancy to preserve cash flow and, in many instances, preserve their lender's confidence in them to pay back their loan.

Tenants who are in a stable position to remain in the property for years to come can take advantage of this opportunity to negotiate an extension of the lease with a reduced rent that is effective immediately. The key word here is "immediately." Not at the end of the lease or at the end of the year, but at the first of the next month.

An offshoot of this idea is an early renewal. Along the same lines of "blend and extend," there may be times when you know you need to remain in the building for longer than the time left on your lease, but your actual lease expiration date is not for two years. You may need to renew it early to secure financing or sell the company, or just to be conservative and lock in the next lease rate before future escalations. In an environment where lease rates are increasing, you may be able to negotiate tomorrow's price today, in exchange for more term to your lease.

I was able to do this for a distribution company I work for in Charlotte, North Carolina. In this instance, my client had a different landlord than the one who had initially leased them the warehouse property eight years earlier. This new landlord had a long-term plan to hold this building in their portfolio. We had one year left, but had recently needed to rebuild some of our key team members, which caused us to delay our plans for a larger warehouse. We instead negotiated a modest future rent increase in a market that was likely to have twice the future market rent growth. We then were able to get the landlord to replace several interior and exterior doors and upgrade all the warehouse lighting to modern LED motion-sensor lights at the time of signing.

CHANGE OF PROPERTY OWNERSHIP

At the most fundamental level, a change of ownership adds another party to the agreement that was not present during the initial negotiations. There are times when nothing changes except for the property manager and life goes on. However, a new landlord is usually a sign of change to come.

When you hear your property is going to be sold, you might want to be on the lookout for the following:

- The new landlord making significant renovations
- A substantial increase in rent
- An increase in property taxes
- New property management
- Different leasing protocols
- Different level of service to the property

The biggest suggestion I can give with a new landlord is to make sure you understand your lease and what you are due. The most common items of an existing lease that are accidently omitted are outstanding debits and credits on lease anniversary dates, such as security deposit credits and free rent credits.

A change of ownership does not have to be all bad, though. One example is the $16 billion Prologis acquisition of Liberty Property Trust. One of my favorite clients was a tenant of Liberty Property Trust. Instead of having a modest portfolio of potential properties to relocate to for our next lease term, we ended up with ten times the opportunities because Prologis maintains 2.5 million square feet in that market. Additionally, Prologis might be disposing of a few assets in this market to balance out their portfolio in the future. This can spell opportunity for my client to buy their facility instead of leasing it.

CAM RECONCILIATION

Executives are often surprised when their landlord sends them a reconciliation statement, then asks for a check to cover last year's increases in property tax, insurance, and maintenance. We call these CAM (common area maintenance) reconciliations or "CAM recs." While they are normal in the commercial real estate world, the size and type of operating expense pass-throughs are not always what they seem.

One third-party logistics client of mine in Fullerton, California, had a lease that stated the landlord was responsible for landscaping costs. However, the landlord told the tenant they could take care of landscaping if they wanted, and the landlord would remove that expense from their bill. It never happened, though. The landlord had a large portfolio of properties, pooled all of their costs, and was not able to remove this expense from one individual property after all. The client paid a landscaping bill twice each month for years before they even noticed. After they called me for help, we were able to negotiate a lease extension on their 50,000-square-foot warehouse that forgave the expense and converted their triple net lease to a gross lease, which is almost unheard of in today's age of institutional landlords.

Another warehousing client of mine leased a 25,000-square-foot industrial building in San Antonio, Texas, within a mixed-use business park that included a few R&D buildings with greater than 25 percent office space. In this particular municipality, the county tax assessor used the office space as a reason to classify the entire business park as a research and development park and assessed it at a higher tax rate. It was only through the client's and my collective review that we were able to figure this out, contrast it with other landlords' property tax bills, and use it to negotiate a favorable relocation.

A third client in Huntington Beach, California, received a bill from a new landlord that was going through a large-scale renovation of the property. Part of the capital expenses were being inadvertently classified as operating expenses and passed on to the tenants. We were able to parse through each operating expense to identify the double billing and obtained an immediate refund and credit to the following month's rent.

In all three cases, only a thorough review of the reconciliation bill brought these topics to the foreground.

Most leases allow for some form of a review of the landlord's books (called "audit rights"), but sometimes limit who can review the books. It can be the tenant, the tenant's broker, the tenant's accountant, or a CPA firm specializing in lease audits. If there is no mention of "audit rights" in the lease, then it is up to you to approach the landlord and determine a reasonable solution.

There can be risk in contesting CAM reconciliations, just like there is risk in baseball arbitration in fair market value litigation. In the lease audit process, the outcome may result in the landlord owing you for accidental or malevolent overcharges. But it can also result in an under-accounting and an additional bill to your company. Think through whether it is worth your time and effort to fight potential discrepancies before you take action.

In the industrial real estate realm, the room for aggressive management of expenses and human error is less pervasive than in the office leasing world, but still possible. If you play the game long enough, you will come across discrepancies. Here is how you should look at these reconciliations:

1. Review your prior CAM reconciliation bills and chart them in a spreadsheet to look for trends and discrepancies in each expense category. Look for scale of magnitude inconsistencies, then annual increase discrepancies.
2. Ask your broker for industry standards for operating expenses. With my experience, I can provide ballpark costs for property management, HVAC, paint, carpet, insurance, office build-out, and sprinkler retrofits off the top of my head.

3. Ask your broker to procure a copy of the BOMA's annual operating expense benchmark report. This report is aggregated by all property managers across the country in office, industrial, and retail real estate. This report is a great way to validate your concern and justification to audit.

Being aware of these discrepancies will give you the proper lens to evaluate each bill and determine whether or not challenging the reconciliation is a worthy endeavor.

KEY TAKEAWAYS

Real estate is a lifelong learning opportunity for executives, and there are always ways to improve. Knowing how to handle moving into a new building, making adjustments, and dealing with common issues is empowering. Knowing your rights and reviewing them annually will help you scrutinize bills you receive from your landlord, and you can utilize your broker to locate the necessary resources to reconcile them. All of this keeps you in the driver's seat, actively managing your real estate, rather than reacting.

We will now shift our focus to how companies of scale operate their real estate. The goal is to provide a benchmark standard so you can create the right environment for continued growth.

CHAPTER 13

ACHIEVING SCALE

As you scale your business, you have the opportunity to scale the way you operate and manage your real estate as well. This scale means something different to each company, based on their ownership structure, capital stack, size, trajectory, skillset, and vision. I have helped clients across the country of every shape and size. The right real estate strategy can have an outsized impact on the trajectory of your business as you scale.

While executive approval of real estate decisions never goes away, the day-to-day responsibilities and management often do. As businesses scale, it is more common to have a corporate real estate director, real estate manager, general manager, or VP with a similar title handle all of the company's real estate. This person can either be the sole person responsible within their company or be part of a small team. This team usually then reports to the CEO or CFO, depending on the company structure.

SINGLE POINT OF CONTACT

The first thing that most executives consolidate when they scale is broker relationships. Having one broker located in every market seems like a good idea, but it is not enough. You do not want to have to explain to each broker everything about your organization's inner workings, vision, and objectives. It takes time and experience to learn your preferences on communication, negotiation style, and personality. It pays to have one broker become a single point of contact for your company and then go about managing all of your local brokerage relationships. It is not that having a local broker is not important; it is quite the contrary. The issue is, managing local brokers is not usually of strategic value to executives as they scale their businesses.

In my experience, companies that have between ten and one hundred locations usually gravitate toward a single broker who demonstrates an aptitude and capability for multi-market brokerage. Anecdotally, this makes up less than 10 percent of brokers nationwide.

It takes time to understand how to scale, from a broker perspective. The first benefit of having the right multi-market broker is that they know how to create a successful working relationship with top talent in each market. There is always a push-pull relationship between who does what, who reports to whom, and when. The broker who understands this concept will take ownership of each assignment in every market, ensure all of their local partners have aligned incentives and expectations, and communicate early and often with their client and local brokers alike.

Your main point of contact is aware of what each local broker needs to know to be effective and can best communicate with them to make sure they are informed to do the best job possible. Your primary point of contact has the benefit of years of experience and knowing what works for you and what does not. This experience then begins to compound, saving you time and leading to better solutions as your relationship strengthens.

There is usually an event that creates the opportunity to consolidate to a single point of contact. Such events are new management hires, retirements, promotions, mergers, acquisitions, and reorganizations. There are also different methods of centralized and decentralized decision-making, where some leaders will have their local managers take care of their real estate and retain approval rights, whereas others will keep all real estate authority in their corporate office.

My company excels in helping clients level up their commercial real estate operations while retaining the entrepreneurial spirit that helped them grow in the first place. An example is with one client I have worked with for the last decade. They have twenty locations across the country in most major markets. We usually have two to three active real estate projects per year. We speak quarterly and are constantly scenario planning for different locations. I work with the CEO, CFO, general counsel, VP of finance, and multiple different levels of territory managers, general managers, and facility managers.

The main benefit to working as a single point of contact for this client can be summed up in the book *The Speed of Trust*, by Stephen Covey. The premise is that when you build a bridge of trust within a relationship, you can increase the speed at which you have high-level engagement to make informed decisions. With the national client example above, we are able to work through multiple different challenging assignments simultaneously. This is, in large part, due to our continued open and honest communication and respect for each other's values and skillsets. Since we have worked together in this capacity for such a long time, we are able to use our complementary knowledge and shared experience in each market in which we do business.

LEASE MANAGEMENT AND TECHNOLOGY SOLUTIONS

Lease management is one of the first areas where growing companies reach a ceiling of complexity. Imagine having two kids. It is possible to keep track of their school schedules, sporting events, community functions, and friends. Now imagine you had ten, twenty, or one hundred kids. One hundred kids sounds crazy, right? In many ways, this is what it is like for growing companies with complex real estate needs. Fortunately, industrial real estate does not require the day-to-day management that kids do, but there are genuine consequences with a poorly managed real estate portfolio.

Andrew Flint, co-founder of the preeminent lease management service firm Occupier, elaborates:

> "The key to proper lease management is a tool that all key stakeholders can access easily. For some of our clients, this is not only the real estate team, but executives, HR, IT, business unit leads, finance, legal, and third-party vendors like brokers, architects, attorneys, accountants, and auditors. The key is to have a single source of data. The problem with legacy tools is they often have poor design and are difficult to use, which leads to apathy and poor adoption. Adding to that challenge, most legacy systems do not facilitate the integration of outside advisors who may need to access some or all of your lease data."

For example, one company I worked with is in the energy business in Newport Beach, California. They had fifty locations across the country and had one person in charge of managing all real estate. This real estate manager had no prior commercial real estate experience and was learning as he went along. I am not against being self-made, but it does help to have the right skillset to get the job done. As time went by and the company grew, he began to receive notices from landlords that they had missed key contract dates to renew leases and had missed termination dates. In one instance, the company had to pay a 200 percent rent penalty for having missed a renewal date. Sadly, their disorganization in real estate matters was symptomatic of company-wide turmoil. The client ended up replacing many of their executives and outsourcing its non-core-business functions.

Often, the shift to a centrally managed lease management database happens when the company hires an executive who has experience working with a lease management system. It is tough for most executives to recognize they have a need to implement a system on their own. Sometimes it is after the insistence of the company's trusted broker. Brokers are continually working with different lease management systems and testing new ones to provide the best available resources for their clients.

When it comes to lease administration, the critical six steps to collecting real estate portfolio information are:

1. Portfolio discovery
2. Assembling all raw data and systems
3. Setting data standards and populating the new system
4. Verification and validation of data
5. Establishing reporting standards
6. Technology delivery and training

When dealing with data, it is easy to conceptually understand the need to consolidate data sets into a central system, but it can oftentimes be more difficult due to lack of standardization, missing documentation, and apathy toward learning a new system. Each step of the process ensures the finished system will report the most impactful and coherent information back to executives through intuitive dashboards. We routinely partner with third-party lease management systems to help clients make the transition as smooth as possible.

While every company has its unique blend of legacy systems, from paper leases to Excel spreadsheets, we find that all benefit from being aggregated, standardized, and digitized. When it comes to third-party software providers, there can be ten to twenty different options at any given point in time. Just like the property selection process is tailored to the client, the technology solution is, as well.

PORTFOLIO OPTIMIZATION

Once our brokerage team has effectively built a database of your company's commercial real estate, we can provide a full portfolio analysis. The foundation for this is the company's vision for the future. When we understand the overarching goals of the executives, we use this to chart a course toward portfolio optimization.

Most companies have inflection points in their growth trajectory that require adjustments to their real estate on a portfolio level. Mergers and acquisitions commonly produce multiple facilities that are redundant or in need of consolidation. This consolidation of facilities is prevalent with private equity firms and larger parent companies. Offshoring, nearshoring, and reshoring are industry-specific portfolio changes that can frequently be related to legislation, economic incentives, and outside events. Additionally, a change in management can often lead to broad initiatives, new product launches, and expansion. Or it can lead to cost cutting, new standards, and consolidation.

Portfolio optimization begins with a review of all the existing operations and real estate documents. With each lease, we go through financial analysis, local market knowledge, market forecasts, real estate responsibilities, occupancy analysis, national market trends, and operational analysis. For industry-specific firms, we may layer on additional considerations such as pallet positions and unit counts, throughput key performance indicators (KPIs), inventory levels, and shipping schedules. Trusted material handling partners are often a consistent presence in these conversations to help advise how each building's warehouse operations will need to adjust, along with property-specific adjustments.

The result of careful portfolio-wide analysis is that we can then build a multistage implementation roadmap, using it to work with the client to adjust each office and industrial space in a measured and methodical manner.

TRANSACTION MANAGEMENT

This book provides you with a framework to think through one single industrial transaction. Reproducing this process at scale is called transaction management.

We work with our clients to build out a unique transaction management process. Our commitment to this process provides us with the capabilities to go out into the marketplace and deliver consistent results. Some obvious benefits are financial and result in the minimization of real estate costs. In contrast, other benefits are intangible, such as improved workplace culture, the ability to forecast farther into the future, or the confidence to press on with growth initiatives.

While each process will have variations depending on the company's needs, generally we follow these eight steps:

1. Audit existing leases: Each agreement has its own set of terms, rights, clauses, and dates that must be understood.
2. Analyze existing floor plan and site plan: Each industrial building has its unique characteristics, as does each operation. Analyzing the relationship between the two can help us understand what is within our control to improve.
3. Interview the local business unit teams: We want to understand their local culture and workflow, and how they align with corporate objectives.
4. Analyze market conditions and landlord relationships: We examine how the current lease agreement or owned property fits within the submarket context and provide market forecasts.
5. Select local broker: We create a list of the region's best talent within our network, utilizing our sixty offices, our existing best-in-class relationships, as well as industry associations like SIOR. We have the flexibility to work with an existing broker relationship or select a new best-in-class broker as desired.
6. Determine the best option: We vet all potential property options and outcomes to formulate a specific strategy.
7. Engage local broker: We work with our local broker to customize our market strategy with local market tactics, ensuring an optimal outcome.

8. Execution: We drive the process with all parties until we have successfully reduced costs, maintained culture, and enhanced the client's business.

When it comes to local broker selection, it is helpful to point out there are multiple ways in which we can optimize this process. For example, I am the single point of contact for one national client, and they provide me with an introduction to their local brokers if they wish for me to work with them. With another client, they allow me to select all the local brokers. I am always sensitive to clients' existing relationships and do my best to keep all existing relationships intact when possible. I have found it can lead to a great outcome where the local team continues to provide valuable service and we are able to learn from each other.

OPEN ARCHITECTURE SOLUTION

The last concept that I will introduce here is the open architecture solution. This basic concept is that we do not dictate whom you use for vendors, such as architects and consultants. In fact, it is just the opposite: we provide you with access to the right vendors and help you select the best one for the matter at hand. We help you choose the best and brightest who can execute in your ideal time frame.

This concept applies to all the resources we have discussed throughout the book: lease audit firms, local brokers, furniture vendors, IT/telecom vendors, project managers, move managers, material handling, supply chain consultants, labor analytics, and site selection firms.

Some brokerage firms restrict their brokers and clients to specific vendors that already have financial relationships with the brokerage. Our firm does not do this and encourages freedom for clients to choose the vendors that best match their needs. Certain firms may not have the right talent across their platform to execute consistently or the network to access all talent. A great book to illustrate this point is Jocko Willink and Leif Babin's *Extreme Ownership: How US Navy Seals Lead and Win*, where they describe the concept of commander's intent. The idea here is that subordinate leaders have the ability to take charge of their smaller teams and can then execute based on a clear understanding of the broader strategy and standard operating procedures. This concept is what empowers our clients to select vendors based on their strengths and ability to execute on the needed assignments.

NEXT STEPS

This completes your executive playbook for industrial real estate leasing. We have gone from high-level strategy down into the weeds of tactical moves of each part of a transaction. We also holistically illustrated how larger organizations operate at scale. Now we will transition into the topic of ownership, as I have found most executives and business owners eventually desire to own and invest in industrial property.

CHAPTER 14

TAKING INVESTMENTS TO THE NEXT LEVEL

This chapter is for the executives who are so fascinated by the industrial property experience that they want to dive in more deeply. You want to take your knowledge and skillsets one step further. You are not content to just lease. Instead, you want to become an investor and buy industrial property. I know this experience firsthand.

My investing career began when my wife and I purchased a three-unit apartment building the month we got married. Few people imagine starting married life in an apartment complex that was constantly under renovation and filled with tenants asking you to fix their toilet at odd hours. However, it turned out to fit us perfectly. We were building our life together, and this was part of the journey.

We decided we loved investing but needed to be more analytical with our next purchase. We were willing to go wherever our analysis took us if we could do so in a safeguarded manner. We looked around the country at demographic shifts, population migration, and job growth. This led us to Austin, Texas. At the time, it seemed like we were gambling, as this was our first experience investing out of state. But Austin has since become a magnet for successful young professionals, and our initial $100,000 investment paid off handsomely—we ended up doubling the amount. The investment was so successful, we invested in Austin again the following year, and the year after that.

When our firm decided to purchase an office building, I invested as a limited partner within the property, while also being a partner in the property's tenant firm. In essence, I was both landlord and tenant. This gave me a better understanding of how to align interests for everyone's benefit.

A year later, it was time to combine my skillset and expertise into industrial investments and build a platform for future investments. In that spirit, we invested in a multi-tenant industrial property in Dallas, Texas. This property acquisition was in a market with growing demographics and job growth during a period of sustained economic expansion, and it was a type of property I knew like the back of my hand. I looked at every investment as an extension of the program and felt comfortable adding value to properties, working with banks, managing property managers, and building relationships with all of my partners.

Today, clients like the fact that I own industrial property. It shows that I practice what I preach. They understand this helps me gain fundamental insights into both sides of the negotiating table. You, too, now have the skills needed to begin managing such an investment prudently. Depending on the scale of your business and its maturity, you may find it is time to invest in buying your industrial property instead of leasing it. Or you might find it is time to start investing in industrial property for retirement or wealth creation, now that you have the capital available.

Figuring out what to invest in is half the battle. The age-old answer is, invest in whatever works for you. I will walk you through the different types of industrial investments in this chapter. Entire books are devoted to investing, but I want to focus on four of the most common investments for entry-level and high-net-worth investors.

OWNER/USER

The term "owner/user" refers to a business that both owns and uses the building. It is the simplest first step toward ownership for executives. Most small businesses initially lease 1,000 to 10,000 square feet of space until they reach stable size and profitability; then they decide it is time to own instead of lease.

Companies that buy their first building for their business usually get a bank loan. Anecdotally, 75 percent of these buyers utilize Small Business Administration (SBA) loans, and 25 percent use conventional financing. When you buy your building for your business, you typically borrow money with a down payment of 10 to 25 percent, amortized in twenty-five years and paid off in twenty-five years.

Owner/user buildings offer security for a bank for a few reasons. The first is because the owner signs a lease with his own business in the space. This alignment of interests means the owner has skin in the game. Additionally, banks also like SBA loans because of how they are structured. The down payment for most industrial property buyers utilizing an SBA loan is as little as 10 percent of the purchase price. I helped my local veterinarian purchase his building with no down payment, using an SBA property loan from a bank that specialized in banking for veterinarians.

SBA loans are actually a composite of two loans. The first loan is for 30 to 40 percent of the purchase price and is the portion lent by the SBA. The second loan, for the remaining balance, is lent by a conventional bank. The SBA is happy because they are promoting small business growth and ownership, and the conventional bank is happy to limit their loan value to 50 percent of the property purchase price. This gives them a lower risk profile.

Typical amortization for these types of loans is twenty-five years. The loan is also due in twenty-five years. Interest rates are fixed for some of that time, before being adjusted every five years at regular intervals.

If you choose to pay off your loan before the first three years, you will be subject to a prepayment penalty. Prepayment penalties provide stability for bank loan portfolios since many banks keep smaller commercial real estate loans on their books.

A conventional loan has many of the same terms, but with a larger deposit that usually represents 25 to 35 percent of the purchase price. Loan fees are generally 1 to 2 percent of the loan amount and are negotiable, depending on the bank.

Loan brokers are a borrower's best friend. A loan broker's job is to know all lenders in the market, shop your loan to the most relevant banks, and negotiate favorable loan terms for you. You can do it yourself too, but I have found the best results occur when working with a loan broker, because there are too many banks in this space to keep up with which one is the best fit. The application process is also time-consuming.

Industrial properties do not come with a warranty period, so it is important to hire an inspector to walk the property and provide an inspection report that will detail every nook and cranny. You must take ownership of the inspection process too: verify everything with your own eyes. Or, better yet, have vendors review your inspection report in hand to give you a real assessment of what it will cost to bring deficient items up to snuff.

Inspectors offer packages that differ in their level of detail. More thorough packages estimate the remaining useful life of all the building components. The most detailed packages include budget line-item costs for each building system. The budgets can help you prioritize big-ticket building systems when negotiating seller credits.

Your bank will require you to have a qualified consultant complete a Phase I study for the property. This involves researching environmental regulatory agency public databases to find out if there are any active or past environmental concerns. This report will usually tell you if the property had underground storage tanks, the status of their removal, and in many cases, if there was soil remediation at the time of removal. The report may also tell you if any unsafe chemicals were used at the site and if they were publicly monitored and disclosed. Some chemicals are susceptible to leaking into the slab and contaminating the soil and groundwater. Banks require reports so they have a full picture of the property and the risks associated with it, because if you do not repay your loan and the bank seizes the property, any environmental issue will be *their* problem.

EXTENDING YOUR INVESTMENT

Purchasing a building that is both an investment and a place of business faces a number of unique considerations.

Most CPAs suggest the building be in a separate LLC. The general purpose is to maximize your company's tax savings with the company lease, while maximizing the executive's personal income tax savings by owning the property. This allows the company to write off its lease payments, property tax, insurance, and maintenance expenses. The executive's building ownership entity can then depreciate the property improvements, write off the interest paid on the loan, and ensure the tenant effectively pays down the mortgage, resulting in cash flow and property appreciation.

In this instance, you are both landlord and tenant. There is always a dichotomy and a healthy tension regarding the rental payment the company makes to its landlord. This moment of stress is where transparency and open discussion between the business owners and the building owners are necessary to determine if there are differing ownership percentages between the two entities.

I usually see the owner/user model as a practice run. Once you invest in your first building and the benefits become clear, you may want to turn these skills into a larger investment strategy.

In a perfect world, the business owner would be able to keep the first building and buy the next, larger building when their business grows to the next size. The older, smaller building would be put on the market for lease and leased out to a new tenant. There are many different variations of this scenario. Another typical example that works well for business owners is continually trading up to a larger building as the business grows.

Eventually, many business owners decide it is time to sell their business. When they do this, they can sell the company and keep the building. Business owners consider this the perfect retirement: they can move on from the day-to-day management of the company and have passive income from a tenant they are intimately familiar with.

I have seen this play out with business owners in buildings ranging from 5,000 square feet to more than 100,000 square feet. The only limit to the size of the outcome is the scale of the business and the ultimate footprint the business needs to be successful.

I worked with a former owner of an apparel manufacturing business that operated out of several facilities in multiple markets within the United States. Upon selling his business, he found his industrial building investments paid more dividends than the business itself. In true entrepreneurial form, he raised private equity funds to scale his industrial investment business, which he still operates today.

Acquiring and managing industrial real estate requires a specific skillset. Once you have developed this skillset, you can put your craft to work and create value in the marketplace.

MULTI-TENANT BUSINESS PARK

This type of industrial investment is a great starting point for the early-stage investor. These properties are called incubator parks, business parks, business centers, industrial parks, or multi-tenant industrial parks. Think of these as apartment complexes of the industrial real estate asset class. Projects can vary from one 10,000-square-foot building up to a large project encompassing multiple buildings totaling 300,000 square feet. Typically, these buildings provide multiple small spaces for startups and local service businesses, ranging from 1,000 to 5,000 square feet per unit.

Multi-tenant projects provide for income-stream diversification. Compare this with the earlier example of a single-tenant building where you either have cash flow or you do not. With investment in a multi-tenant project, you have five to fifty tenants producing income, but no single tenant makes up more than 5 to 10 percent of the project. Of course, the tradeoff for this steady stream of income is an increase in management duties. Managing twenty leases means there is more of a need for a property manager, common area maintenance, HVAC maintenance, and enhanced tenant relations.

Smaller tenants are usually less sophisticated and less capitalized, and may not be able to weather a down market, a challenging business environment, or credit crunches. Smaller tenants typically sign shorter leases too, ranging from two to three years in length, as they have less visibility into their future than larger, more mature businesses. That means that you might have 25 to 50 percent of your tenant leases expiring each year. Marketing smaller spaces, cleaning and prepping each space when vacant, and screening new tenants all take time and money.

There is an upside to this, though. With a five-year lease on a larger building, market lease rates might go up at 8 percent each year, but your contract fixes the increase at 3 percent increases. With shorter-term leases, you are better able to keep your lease rate increases consistent with market rate increases.

Buying multi-tenant industrial property means a larger down

payment, usually 20 to 40 percent down. It is common to have your interest rate fixed for five years at a time, with periodic adjustments to market rate.

You must be aware of the debt coverage ratio, which is the amount of net income the property produces divided by your estimated debt payment. The purpose of this debt coverage ratio is to make sure the property economics are robust enough to pay the loan back even in the event of unexpected expenses, loss of revenues, deterioration of market demand, or an increase in the supply of competitive properties. It can fluctuate but usually hovers around 1.25. This means that the property has to generate 25 percent more revenue than the debt service due each month.

Amortization rates for these properties are usually twenty years but can sometimes be twenty-five years. A twenty-year amortization differs from the traditional thirty-year fixed-rate residential mortgage in that the principal loan balance decreases more rapidly.

Due to the fact that commercial income property loans have shorter maturity dates, you have to refinance more often or be willing to sell and exchange property more frequently than you would with residential income property. This can lead to financing challenges if a five- or ten-year loan matures during unfavorable market conditions. You want to make sure you set up your investment strategy to weather down markets and never put yourself in a position where your property is worth less than your loan balance.

Your motivation to scale will determine what you do at these financing junctures:

1. You can sell the property every time your loan is due, pay the taxes, and keep the cash liquid for future investments.

2. You can refinance the loan and continue to pad your property's operating account. You will then decide how much additional principal you want to pay down.
3. More aggressive investors will refinance back up to the maximum loan value and take out proceeds to reinvest in another property. This is a winning strategy because the money you pull out of the property is tax-free.

SINGLE-TENANT NET

The third type of industrial investment is the single-tenant net leased (STNL) investment. These investments can often be great for conservative investors who prioritize stable, long-term cash flow over maximizing returns. These investors usually look for a safe harbor to park their funds at an attractive rate, with all the tax benefits of ownership. The quintessential example here would be buying a warehouse leased to FedEx for the next ten years.

There are dozens of factors that impact the pricing of an STNL property. The primary factors are length of lease term, credit, the cap rate, and the geographic area where the property is located.

An example of how the length of lease term affects the property can be shown with an industrial property with three years versus fifteen years left on the lease. If you need a loan on a property with a three-year lease, you will likely find you can only get a three-year loan, which may not be consistent with your long-term hold strategy. On the other hand, if you need a loan on a property with a fifteen-year lease, you will be able to obtain a longer loan maturity, which could dramatically affect your cash flow and down payment.

Secondary considerations are property characteristics, submarket demographics, and your ability to lease the property in the future. If you have a fifteen-year lease and plan on holding on to the property for five to seven years, you might not delve as heavily into all the factors that would be relevant to future leasing. If you are in the game long enough, like one of my clients who owns nine single-tenant industrial buildings, you realize you will eventually need to have a tenant move out of your property, and at that time, you will need to hire a broker to market your property for lease. At that time, it is imperative for you to have a functional building in a growing area. While vacancy has been at a historical low for the past decade, some buildings have sat vacant on the market for months, even years, at a time. Anyone who has been through that experience has a more discerning eye for property and market analysis.

Single-tenant net leased investments are simple, low-risk, and generate moderate returns. Triple net leases are set up so the tenant is responsible for paying all of the property tax, insurance, and maintenance on the property, as if they owned it. If they have a long-term lease, you will be freed up to use your time as you see fit, rather than managing tenants, property managers, and real estate attorneys.

SALE-LEASEBACK

The last popular industrial real estate investment with high-net-worth individuals is the sale-leaseback. The only difference between the single-tenant net leased industrial investment and a sale-leaseback is that the company selling the building is the property's tenant. Sale-leasebacks are generally pursued by experienced investors, as there is more room for creativity in structuring the transaction to be mutually beneficial.

Companies look at sale-leasebacks as a financing instrument: investors in sale-leasebacks will underwrite the company, much like a banker would. If you are thinking of purchasing a building in this situation, find out why the company is trading their ownership stake for capital and what they intend to do with this newfound capital. Usually, you will find that the company is reorganizing and needs the funds to pay off debt and/or focus on acquisitions.

One sale-leaseback I listed and sold recently in Tustin, California, was for a printing company. This printing company had been in business for twenty years and in the same warehouse for the last ten years. The printing industry, however, has been going through massive consolidation due to the prominence of digital media, so printing companies have had to be nimble and adjust. This is difficult for a business that requires substantial capital investment in the form of large-format machines. Printing companies that once just printed mailers have had to diversify their services to include packaging for cosmetics, craft beer, cannabis, and other new growth industries. My client was trying to become more vertically integrated by adding a digital marketing agency. To fuel this growth, they decided to sell their building and then lease it back from the buyer.

Other considerations in a sale-leaseback are the length of the lease term, capital improvements, and security deposit. Remember, you are not just buying a building: you are also signing a lease with the seller. This means you need to put your landlord hat on and consider a mutually agreeable lease term; the condition of the property, roof, and HVAC units; and how to handle the amount and payment of a security deposit.

Sometimes the seller will want to maximize proceeds, which

means they will offer the lowest cap rate possible to maximize the property value. Buyers, on the other hand, usually want to increase their cap rate by offering a lower purchase price.

INVESTOR SKILLSET

Combinations and permutations of investment strategies organically take place in industrial markets. For example, I recently worked with a high-net-worth couple who had long since retired and wanted to spend more time fishing and traveling to Mexico. They had initially purchased a small industrial building to occupy as an owner/user.

Over the next ten-year period, they turned their owner/user investment into a multi-tenant investment by using the extra land on their office property to build an industrial building that consisted of five units. Each unit had an entrance, reception area, private office, restrooms, water, power, and a roll-up door. The couple leased out all of these units and kept them leased for years, which effectively paid their mortgage on the front part of the building. During this time, they managed everything themselves: leasing, bookkeeping, maintenance, contracts, and more.

After a few more years went by, they asked me to do their leasing, and they requested I find a property manager to take care of the day-to-day operations. A few years later, they decided to sell the property. We sold it to an owner/user who needed all of the building units for his own business.

My clients were able to take the money from the property sale and buy a newly constructed, single-tenant net leased building with a fifteen-year lease in Dallas, Texas.

When we met, this couple was generating $27,576 of net cash flow every year from an old 1960s industrial building. Following my advice, they ended up with an investment that generated $96,000 of net cash flow in year one and is set to compound 3 percent annually for the next fifteen years.

These investors moved up the investment food chain over the years. They started as owner/user investors, became multi-tenant industrial investors, and ended up being single-tenant net lease investors. Today, they are hard to reach because they spend their time enjoying retirement, just as they had hoped. All of their accounts are direct deposit because this couple only checks their mail when they are back in the United States once a month.

The moral of this chapter is that leasing, owning, and managing industrial real estate is a valuable skillset. You can use these skills, if you so desire, to create successful investments for yourself, your business, your family, and your retirement.

CONCLUSION

It is in service as my role as an advisor that I seek to elevate the conversation around the commercial real estate market and improve the experience of my clients, colleagues, the community, and you, the reader of this book.

For me, commercial real estate began as just a job. I needed to learn the mechanics of a real estate transaction so I could build a business. Over the years, I have recognized that this business is a blessing that allows me to collaborate with deep thinkers to solve complex problems and to contribute to the success of thousands of people.

Writing this book has taught me about commitment and courage in unexpected ways. It has helped me to organize my thoughts, catalog my experience, and tease out lessons learned along the way.

My hope is that you are able to use this book to take action, create new ideas, clarify your thinking, share experiences, and make a positive impact in your company so you can thrive.

Let me be a resource to you. I would like to have a discussion about the challenges within your organization and collaborate with you in the future. Connect with me on LinkedIn, or send an email to jbsmith@leeirvine.com with the subject "Book," and I will add you to my monthly newsletter that discusses current events in our space.

Thank you for the opportunity to be of service to you.